Mending and repair in a throwaway world

Foreword by Jay Blades

Katie Treggiden

Ludion

A mighty community showing up in this moment, gathering the pieces of a broken world and doing the work of mending.

– Ayana Elizabeth Johnson and Katharine Wilkinson[1]

Foreword

As far as I'm concerned, Katie Treggiden is my fairy godmother. In the early 2010s, I launched the charity Out of the Dark, trying to bring redesign and repurposing to the masses, training young people who didn't necessarily have a chance at school to make money through repair. Katie was one of our earliest champions – she connected us to the design world, which I knew nothing about. Katie was my guru – she knew everybody! Today, I say to people: if you're working in craft, design or the circular economy, and Katie doesn't know what you're doing, then you're probably not doing it right.

The charity didn't last – it folded in 2015 – but my admiration for Katie and the work she does has continued to this day. She has an amazing ability to unite people, to bring them together into this brilliantly *unfashionable* way of living that she is helping to create.

I say 'unfashionable' because not enough people have accepted the fact that we urgently need to move away from the consumerist society that we've found ourselves in. Our planet simply cannot sustain this culture of 'buy it, break it, chuck it' anymore. Many people find that hard to accept – or they don't want to because they're part of the 1% who benefit from things staying as they are. But we have to change things; we have to think about what we're leaving our grandchildren on this planet, the mess that we're expecting them to clear up. That can be scary to think about, so we don't think about it. Thinking these things, saying them out loud, calling for change, just isn't trendy.

Broken is not a trendy book. A trendy book – a *fashionable* book – would be about new designs. Because our society has conditioned us to believe that old things, worn things, broken things, have less or no value compared to new ones. Advertising tells us to BUY NOW! And, in six months' time, BUY AGAIN! Repair is the opposite of that. If we all repaired our broken things, the commercial world would grind to a halt.

And they know this. As Katie explains in 'Repair as restoration of function' (p. 12), products such as smartphones are often engineered to fail within a set time frame – 'planned obsolescence' is a feature of their manufacture and often their marketing strategy too. Repair is discouraged by closing the object off so you can't physically get into it to fix it, and even if you could, the company's warranty tells you that you mustn't – it's against their rules. At the same time, we have tied the cycle of consumption to our social status. There's a reason new trainers get released at the beginning of the school year: to make kids hungry for the cred that the new pair will give them, and to make last year's pair less valuable, less worth keeping. In so many ways, consumerism pits us all against each other in competition for the new.

Things are made to be replaced, not repaired, because that is the most profitable approach for the corporation, and any business navigating a globalist, capitalist society has to prioritise growth above everything else in order to survive. Repair is therefore inherently anti-capitalist – and, as 'Repair as activism' (p. 94) shows, it can even be interpreted as an act of rebellion. To stand up and say: 'Don't throw that away, repair it – and if you don't have the skills to fix it, find someone in the community who does and who can share that knowledge with you' is not the trendy thing to do – but maybe it will be in future.

Our TV show, *The Repair Shop*, has been hugely successful, watched by millions of people all over the world. The rise of *The Repair Shop* came during the height of the Covid pandemic. This was a time when many of us were looking out for our neighbours, clapping for the NHS, thinking about our impact on other people – it was a time when we were rediscovering our sense of community.

I don't think that's a coincidence. There is a powerful relationship between repair and community, as Katie explores in 'Repair as healing' (p. 138). By its very nature, repair connects us to the past – both our own history and the stories we share with our families, our neighbours and the places we come from. When we fix something, we're putting value back into that object, but we're also preserving the memories it holds and the stories it tells. That's why people find *The Repair Shop* so emotional; those memories and stories might only mean something to that object's owner, but as a viewer you instinctively understand the parallel with your own experiences and the stories held in your own objects. It reminds us that we're all part of something a bit bigger than ourselves, and it reconnects us to the tradition of community skills being passed down from generation to generation. Where the disposability-driven culture of consumerism keeps us apart, repair brings us back together. It's healing, and it's powerful.

To me then, *Broken* is fundamentally a book about community. Every one of the makers, menders, artists and craftspeople featured – whether they're using repair to fix something physically broken or as a way to process profound emotional trauma – understands that repair is a conversation with the past, and an act of care for the future. This is what I call the 'historical future' – taking something from history and redesigning it, giving it a new future in the process. That is what the people in this book are doing, and it is also what *Broken* itself does. Taken together, the examples of repair in these pages map our way forward – a route to a better tomorrow for our planet and our society, for ourselves and our grandchildren.

Getting there is not going to be easy. It's painful to say, but the people that should read this book probably won't. I don't know whether society at large will take on board the lessons in these chapters, whether they'll follow the examples of the people in these pages. I hope they do. I hope they read this book and watch *The Repair Shop* and change the way they think about the things around them, whether it's a broken toaster or a damaged family heirloom.

Because the fact is our current system *is* broken, and – this might be the only time I ever make this suggestion – it could well be time to replace it altogether.

Jay Blades
London, January 2023

Introduction – a case for paying attention

Broken [adjective] – damaged, no longer able to work; interrupted or not continuous; (of a person) having given up all hope; despairing[1]

... other things can be repaired. Objects, of course. Traditions can be. Hope can be. Emotions eventually. But it requires cautious handling, patience and care. Old hope can age beautifully.

– Otto von Busch[2]

I am writing this in the searing heat of July 2022. Temperatures in the UK have exceeded 40°C for the first time in history,[3] railway lines are warping, runways are melting,[4] and people across Europe are dying.[5] I live in a county famous for its 'mizzle' (a portmanteau of 'mist' and 'drizzle') and I drove home past a wildfire this afternoon. In this moment, while I acknowledge the privilege that make these new experiences for me, I understand more clearly than ever before that our systems and structures are broken. The planet is heating up. It's time to move away from a linear take-make-waste economy, away from the three Cs of capitalism, colonialism and consumerism, and away from the idea of human supremacy over the natural world – before it's too late.

And yet our news cycles have been filled, not with dire warnings and calls for change, but with abandoned net-zero commitments, fossil fuel companies announcing off-the-chart profits, and puff pieces about people going to the beach to take advantage of the hot weather. Clearly the system is working just fine for some.

The question of who gets to decide what is broken and what gets repaired or remade is at the heart of this book. Author, activist and social justice facilitator Adrienne Maree Brown argues that our work is to 'notice what is broken, clean up the dangerous fragments of the past, and let them go – or remake them into something beautiful, and then begin again'.[6] First, we have to notice what is broken.

Despite the lack of coverage in mainstream news, most of us understand that we are living in the age of the Anthropocene and that human activity is now the dominant influence on the climate. We know that we have changed natural ecosystems that have existed on Earth for millennia in ways that can't be reversed; we have lost half the world's biodiversity in my lifetime alone and global temperatures are close to spiralling out of control. And we know that the systems and structures that oppress and exploit the global majority are more than unjust – they are damaging to all but the global elite. We know full well what is broken, it's just that sometimes – often – we can't bear to look. It's too hurtful, too unfair, too frightening, so we look away.

Whichever side of the political divide we fall, we probably also know that it's not finished breaking yet. 'These systems of oppression will inevitably fall,' says Brown. 'The structures that are not compatible with life on Earth will end.' US academic Steven Jackson agrees: 'Many of the stories and orders of modernity (or whatever else we choose to call the past two-hundred-odd years of Euro-centred human history) are in the process of coming apart, perhaps to be replaced by new and better stories and orders, but perhaps not.'[7] And it's that 'perhaps not' that is key, along with the question: 'better' for whom? Because if we are really honest, we all know that more change is coming – and we're scared. That's why governments seem to be swinging wildly from far left to far right, why oil companies are hoarding profits and why the voices of naysayers, doomsters and conspiracy theorists are getting louder and louder.

If we want new and better stories and world orders – ones that are better for all of us, not just a tiny minority – we can't look away any longer. We need to hold the stare with what is broken, with what can be repaired or remade, and what needs to be cleaned up and let go.

The act of noticing, of paying attention and asking questions, enables us to hold space for two radically different realities – realities that Jackson describes as 'a fractal world, a centrifugal world, an always-almost-falling-apart world' on the one hand, and 'a world in a constant process of fixing and reinvention, reconfiguring and reassembling into new combinations and new possibilities' on the other. He describes our broken world as 'a world of pain and possibility, creativity and destruction, innovation and the worst excesses of leftover habit and power', and suggests that 'the fulcrum of these two worlds is repair: the subtle acts of care by which order and meaning in complex sociotechnical systems are maintained and transformed, human value is preserved and extended, and the complicated work of fitting to the varied circumstances of organizations, systems, and lives is accomplished.'[8]

Broken-world thinking asserts that 'break-down, dissolution, and change, rather than innovation, development, or design as conventionally practised and thought about' are what we need to focus our attention on. Or as Mister Rogers' mum put it, 'Look for the helpers, you will always find people who are helping.'[9] This is a book then, not about designers, innovators and makers, but about menders, repairers, fixers, hackers and remakers – about those helpers: the people who can look damage and decay in the eye and construct new orders; new and better stories.

In a throwaway society, in which most people chose to look away – to replace rather than repair – this book will explore the societal and cultural roles that mending plays. Of course, the restoration of function is one of them, but the objects featured are rarely mended solely for pragmatic reasons. There is usually something in the original damaged piece that would be lost if it were simply replaced, not to mention the heritage craft skills involved in its restoration. 'There are a lot of people who love the materials and the processes,' says Chris Miller in 'Repair as restoration of function' (p. 47). 'I like to think that what we do honours and respects that.' Whether it is harking back to a simpler way of life, or a desire for things made with a quality that is difficult to find in contemporary products, restoration offers more value than replacement – it's just that 'value' is not always measured in financial terms.

In 'Repair as storytelling', we look at repair as a way to retain, retell and reimagine the stories embodied within objects. In her book *Craft of Use*, Kate Fletcher critiques images of fashion garments that are 'unworn, uncrumpled, capturing the idealised moment before a person slips on a piece, before time and life enters the sleeves, marks the collar and creases the fabric at the hip of the trouser leg'.[10] It is the crumples, the marks and the creases – the craft of use – that the artists, menders and remakers who tell stories through repair are interested in: the time and life that those objects have already experienced and the time and life yet to unfold. As Celia Pym says on p. 57: 'I am often more interested in the damage than the repair... Understanding the story behind an object changes its value, makes you appreciate it differently.'

Although any form of mending or repair could be seen as a form of activism in today's single-use culture, many of today's artists, menders and remakers are choosing to make a statement with their work. 'A broken object delivers frustration because it doesn't achieve its functionality,' says Paulo Goldstein on p. 122. 'But the same principle applies to a broken system.' The people profiled in 'Repair as activism' are deliberately using repair to point a finger at what is broken at the systemic, structural and cultural level of society – asking us to notice, to pay attention.

While some are working to raise awareness of the impact of our broken systems, others are quietly working to repair or remake them. The curators and remakers in 'Repair as healing' are all finding ways to heal personal injuries, to reconnect people and to rebuild communities through mending and repair. 'I approach repair as an act of healing,' says Ekta Kaul on p. 144. 'To stitch is to mend feelings of loss, to process emotions, to hold on to memories and to create new connections with what I hold precious.'

Finally, in 'Regeneration as repair', we come to regeneration, because as Sebastian Cox says on p. 214, 'It's essential that we not only try to... stay sustainable, but that we actually try to repair what has been lost.' It is no longer enough to simply repair the things we have already taken from the Earth, we also need to mend the systems we broke in the process of taking them. The people profiled in chapter five are doing exactly this.

And so, despite the context within which I write, despite the systems and structures that are – to my mind – so utterly broken, I am not. I have not given up all hope; I am not yet despairing. I work hard every day to maintain what Christiana Figueres and Tom Rivett-Carnet call 'stubborn optimism' – one of three mindsets they recommend in their book *The Future We Choose* for combatting climate change.[11] Stubborn optimism is not blind faith or naive hope, it is the result of doing the work of holding space for all that is broken, all that might be repaired or remade, and all that needs to be cleaned up and let go. I find hope in the work of those who mend, despite all the reasons not to – the parents, grandparents and caregivers who patch knees worn through children's trousers; the shed-dwellers, allotment keepers and garage owners who can always find something that 'might do'; and the 28 people profiled in this book. I hope they help you to find your way back to stubborn optimism too; to hold space for both the pain and the possibility; to reconnect with old hope and find it has aged beautifully.

Katie Treggiden
Cornwall, July 2022

Note to the reader

The words 'mending' and 'repair' have slightly different meanings and inferred gender and material implications. However, when you write a whole book about a subject, it's handy to have more than one word with which to refer to it, so I will be using the two terms interchangeably in order to maintain textual interest for you, the reader.

Repair as restoration of function

Restoration [noun] – the action of returning something to a former condition, place or owner or the process of repairing or renovating a building or work of art[1]

Age and wear diversify the surfaces of things in ways that nothing else will. If nothing ever lasted, we should be denied that beauty.

– David Pye[2]

The sense of returning to a previous state is perhaps more present in the word 'restore' than in any of the other terms we use for different types of mending and repair. In the 14th century, the verb 'restoren' meant to give back; to build up again or repair; to renew or re-establish; to free from the effects of sin; or to bring back to a former and better state. Later in the same century, 'restoracioun' meant 'a means of healing or restoring health, a cure; renewing of something lost.'[3] And it is the notion of renewing something lost that perhaps most accurately captures what restoration is, because it's rarely as simple as undoing the effects of time. Ecologist Gary Nabhan coined the term 're-story-ation'[4] to highlight the quandary of deciding which of its many stories a restored piece should tell. 'A restoration usually involves a return to some earlier incarnation, but there's very little that is black and white,' says textile artist and former museum conservator Lauren Chang. 'There are times when something gets restored because it has been modified and modified and no longer represents the part of its life that is of most interest, so you might restore it to a more historically significant or culturally relevant period, but it's important to explore who gets to decide that – who holds the power to choose which stories are told.'[5] In more informal restorations, the 'culturally relevant period' of a toaster, for example, might simply be a time when it worked.

But whereas older objects are often *open* and *readable* – that is, you can see how they are made and therefore how they might be mended simply by examining them – the mass-produced *closed* objects from the mid-20th and 21st centuries can be less suggestive of restoration.[6] Co-founder of vintage lighting brand skinflint, Chris Miller (p. 44), talks about the events that bookend the period of time from which he will restore lights. The first, predictably enough, is the advent of mainstream electricity in the 1920s, but there are two factors that determine the most recent pieces he will take on. 'In the 1970s, you get plastics coming into lighting and you start to see the language of planned obsolescence coming into the documentation,' he says. Planned obsolescence refers to the controversial, often denied but no doubt commonplace practice of rendering goods unusable or undesirable within a certain time frame after purchase, to encourage replacement. Tactics include limited battery life, restricted availability of spare parts, non-durable materials – and even frequently changing designs, which render something psychologically if not literally obsolete, raising more questions about who gets to decide what is deemed 'broken'.

Craft theorist David Pye wrote in his 1968 book *The Nature and Art of Workmanship*, 'If you are making a thing so that it goes wrong or breaks, then, however honestly you state the facts, two other facts remain. One is that you are putting as little into the job as you decently can. The other is that you are [forcing] its user to spend his money on replacing that thing instead of for some other purpose.'[7] There are always those who will argue that you can have a go at repairing anything, but, as co-founder of The Restart Project, Janet Gunter, puts it, 'You can pick up that screwdriver, but the system is rigged against you.' The oft-cited example in repair circles is tractors. Farmers have a deep history of thrift and repair. 'Their identities were constructed from things that couldn't be bought in shops,' writes James Rebanks, author of *English Pastoral*, of his grandfather's generation of farmers. 'They wore old clothes... and would mend anything that broke, piling up old things to use again someday, rather than throwing them away.'[8] But today, a tractor costs in the region of £650,000 and, according to some manufacturers, spending that much doesn't even mean you own the thing – you have merely bought an 'implied license for the life of the vehicle to operate the vehicle'.[9] Piggybacking on to the 1998 Digital Millennium Copyright Act (DMCA – US legislation intended to protect software makers from piracy), the makers of these increasingly software-driven machines force farmers to come to them for repairs, instead of using more cost- and time-effective local repair shops or undertaking the work themselves.[10] The cost to farmers is not just the immediate financial outlay, it can also be measured in lost time, income and even livelihoods, as the delays that often result can mean missed harvests and wasted crops. The manufacturers argue that there is a safety risk in allowing anybody to tamper with these increasingly automated and connected machines, but activists for the 'right to repair' are calling for equipment manufacturers to share access to the diagnostic tools, manuals and other supplies that farmers need to fix their own machines – just like the owners of older machines, such as Rebanks' grandfather, could.

Tractor owners – correction: tractor licensees – have met an unlikely set of allies in the tech-savvy tinkerers who believe that a smartphone costing upwards of £750 and containing 16 of the 17 rare earth metals and five different 'conflict minerals'[11] ought to last longer than a year or two. Many smartphones are as locked down as modern tractors and just as difficult to repair – even taking the back off one can render its warranty invalid – and their manufacturers have been lobbying lawmakers in opposition to the 'right to repair' bills that farmers are campaigning for.[12] Smartphone makers argue that such changes in the law could open them up to copyright infringement, result in poor-quality repair work and render consumers vulnerable to hackers. These may all be valid points, but right-to-repair advocates don't believe they are the real motivations behind their determination to keep us from tinkering with our own phones. The smartphone repair market is worth about 1% of the retail market[13] – keeping products in use just isn't profitable. But not being able to keep them in use isn't good for those that buy them. 'There's this pervasive sense that we're ruled by these inscrutable forces that are hard to bring within view,' says Matthew Crawford, author of *Shop Class as Soulcraft*. 'Being able to be the master of your own stuff, to open it up and take a look and take care of it, answers to a very basic human need.'[14]

Addressing this very basic human need, Dutch environmentalist and journalist Martine Postma set up the first Repair Café in Amsterdam in 2009. Within a decade, there were almost 1,700 Repair Cafés in 35 countries around the world.[15] The model is simple: members of the public bring in broken objects and are paired with volunteers with the skills to fix them. But here's the catch: you can't just drop broken objects off – the repair has to be a collaborative effort. 'Things break, and when they do, most people just don't know what to do any more,' says Postma.

> 'They have no repair skills, they have no tools, and no time to focus on the subject. And so, when something breaks, they feel helpless... Repair Café connects people with their common sense and their inner feeling of what's right. When you make the time to make a repair, you realise that it's actually a very normal thing to do... and when you succeed,

it makes you feel strong. It empowers you, and when communities are empowered, they're capable of achieving more together. That's the kind of mindset we need for a more sustainable future.'[16]

It's more than just a mindset shift. The more people get involved in repair and restoration – the more normal a response to a broken object it becomes – the more they start to understand the systemic barriers; the social, economic and environmental systems and structures that limit their agency to mend the things they own. As artist and researcher Jonnet Middleton puts it, 'to experience mending first-hand pushes the mending ethic deep inside our consciousness and rewires our consumer brains.'[17] We suddenly start to question clothes only made to standards that anticipate a five-week lifespan,[18] without the quality, generous seams or button and thread once affixed to every care label that encouraged simple mends. We start to question whether we should have to replace a hermetically sealed smartphone rendered useless by nothing more than a battery that will no longer hold its charge. 'We feel trapped by planned obsolescence,' write John Wackman and Elizabeth Knight in their book *Repair Revolution.* 'Repair culture aims to establish the agency of repair and reuse as social norms, as a way of challenging and remaking the ecology of our economy.'[19] As well as repairing individual objects, many of these groups are campaigning for governments to pass laws that require manufacturers to provide instruction manuals, spare parts and access to enable repairs. 'The products we're seeing... are simply not meant to be repaired,' says Gunter. 'Our volunteers pushed us not just to do these events and deal with the downstream wreckage of a linear economy, but also to try to fix the system.'[20] They are making progress. In 2015, France made planned obsolescence illegal.[21] And in 2021, the UK followed the EU's lead in bringing in the Ecodesign and Energy Labelling Regulations, dubbed the 'right to repair bill', which requires that manufactures make spare parts and maintenance information available for lighting, washing machines, dishwashers, fridges and televisions.[22] These laws don't go far enough, but they are evidence that grassroots action can make a difference.

Chris Miller's lighting brand skinflint (p. 44) is just one of the restoration-based companies explored in this chapter. Rachael South (p. 18) joins Miller in celebrating the craftsmanship of vintage pieces made by those who put more into the job than they could decently get away with – taking pride in a thing made to last. Jude Dennis and Hannah Stanton (p. 36) subvert the norms of traditional upholstery, fighting for its place in the modern era, while Vincent Dassi (p. 30) and Jane ní Dhulchaointigh (p. 24) have both come up with new and innovative solutions to age-old problems. All the remakers in this chapter normalise the idea of keeping materials and objects in use (the second tenet of the circular economy). The more we can all join them in celebrating the 'diversity of surfaces' that only age and wear can bring about, the more we will all start to question products that are built to break – and that can only be a good thing.

Rachael South

Rachael South with wild rushes harvested in Somerset

Michael South was a bare-knuckle boxer from a large Irish community that had originally settled in London in Victorian times. As his boxing career waned, a pedlar's licence meant that he was able to supplement his income caning chairs on the kerbsides of west London. Today, his granddaughter Rachael South (1969, London, UK) might not be much help in a bar brawl, but she is carrying on the tradition of furniture repair – skills she started to learn at just 14 years old, when her father handed down the techniques he had learned from her grandfather. 'My family ran an upholstery and chair caning business, and as children, my sisters and I would go into the workshop with my dad at weekends,' she says. 'I really liked the environment and was a willing assistant to any of the upholsterers who wanted my help. Once dad saw that I had the patience

Weaving a seat with wild rushes harvested in Somerset

to sit and learn this relatively slow craft, he taught me chair caning – and later rush and seagrass weaving – and was soon giving me all the cane chairs to restore. As I grew older, other furniture dealers and upholsterers started to give me their furniture to weave seats for too.'

Whereas chair frames have traditionally been made from wood, from the 1650s onwards the supporting structure of their seats was typically made from woven rattan vine (or less commonly, rush and cane, and, in the 19th and 20th centuries, willow, paper cord, or seagrass) and designed to be repaired and replaced over time. From the late 18th century, chair caners could be found on London street corners, where they would repair chairs for a small fee. As the skillset has declined, a worn-out seat often spells the end of a chair's life. 'I am horrified to think of these chairs ending up in landfill – the idea of repair is built into their design, so how could they be thrown away?' asks South, who, as well as working to commission, runs workshops to pass her skills on to others. 'Chair caners and seat weavers are not common, but there are a few working around the country – and I am pleased to say that I have taught a lot of people, including working upholsterers and furniture restorers,' she says. 'I hope to teach as many as are interested in learning, to ensure a future for my craft.'

South's parents suggested that she joined the family business when she finished school, but, encouraged by her art teacher, she went to London Guildhall University where she studied textile design and then had a successful career as a bespoke passementerie (the trimmings used to embellish soft furnishings) designer. When the time came to set up her own business, she realised her father already had a good business model and she would have the opportunity to add her own creative edge. Today, she is known as the go-to person for all types of seat-weaving restoration, working on everything from fine antiques for private clients and museums to mid-century classics and much-loved chairs that have been in family homes for generations. 'Most of the furniture I work on could not be replaced like for like – they are unique pieces that are not manufactured today,' she says. 'By restoring, that personal connection to the past is assured.'

After almost 40 years of chair caning, she still loves the craft as much as she did all those years ago in her father's workshop. 'The longer I have done this type of work, the more interesting it has become to me,' she says. 'My fascination hasn't waned at all since I first learned when I was young. The furniture I restore is testament to exquisite craftsmanship in both the design and the construction – each piece is a living history of techniques and materials and every one is unique.'

South's motivations are rooted in more than just her personal feelings about the practice. 'I am actively engaged with environmentalism,' she says. 'I use all-natural materials for seat weaving, all of which could be composted once worn out. I am happy to save every chair I work on from landfill – a mindset that seeks to restore rather than replace is crucial for moving forward and facing the climate crisis.'

She believes this message is starting to get through to other people too. 'Restoration is a known thing now and people are aware that they can save an item rather than just throwing it away and buying new,' she says. 'I do think people are much more aware that they can find someone who can restore their furniture for them, or come to a class to restore it themselves.' She is also pleased to see people buying second-hand and vintage furniture for their homes instead of buying new: 'Nowadays, people are more eclectic and will choose second-hand items, and not necessarily because they are valuable antiques. This can only be a good thing – it is essential that we throw less away.'

A mindset that seeks to restore rather than replace is crucial for moving forward and facing the climate crisis.

Rachael South in her workshop in Dalston, east London

Caning a seat (above and opposite)

The furniture I restore is testament to exquisite craftsmanship in both the design and the construction – each piece is a living history of techniques and materials.

Jane ní Dhulchaointigh

'What if it isn't that you're the designer, but that this is a material that turns *everyone* into a designer?' That was the question that unlocked everything for Jane ní Dhulchaointigh (1979, Kilkenny, Ireland), inventor and co-founder of Sugru. Following an undergraduate degree and early work as an artist, she was in the midst of a master's in product design at the Royal College of Art in London when she had an uncomfortable epiphany. 'I was keen to put my creativity to more everyday use through design,' she says. 'I just hadn't connected the dots between design and consumer culture until I started the course. Realising that design can be used to fuel consumer culture and waste was a dark moment for me. But, because the course was so experimental and included a lot of subversive design thinking, I was encouraged to explore that realisation.'

She experimented with materials in the workshop by combining waste wood dust with silicone sealant and came up with a mouldable material that could bond to things. She was using it to adapt and mend things around her student flat, when the lightbulb moment happened. Her then boyfriend, now husband, put it to her that maybe she didn't have to design a fix for consumer culture, perhaps she could instead empower everyone to do what she was doing – adapting and mending the things around them, instead of throwing them away and buying new. 'Bingo!' she says. 'My brain exploded with ideas about a world in which everything could be fixed, hacked or improved and I was hooked! It was then a question of finding people who could help me actually invent the material technology, and that took me on a whirlwind journey into the worlds of science, business and, eventually, manufacturing, sales and purpose-led marketing.'

Twenty years on, Sugru, the 'mouldable glue' that came out of that whirlwind journey, is used by millions of people in 170 countries across the world to adapt and repair countless objects from computer cables to pan handles. Many of them use Sugru to undertake their first repair. Mending is something that comes very naturally to ní Dhulchaointigh. 'My maternal grandmother was a dedicated maker and mender of clothes,' she says. 'She would spend every Sunday at our house and sit by the fire mending for hours. If you didn't have anything for her to mend, she would be crestfallen, so we all kept up a steady supply of socks, jeans or whatever we could find.' Growing up on a farm meant repair was the norm outside the home too. 'On farms, when something breaks or doesn't work very well, you don't go to the shops, you try to fix it or remake it. My dad would regularly have the welder out, building or adapting gates. Structures are always evolving, and it was only when I moved to London as a student that I appreciated how that mindset could be liberating in more urban settings or more fixed ways of thinking about our belongings.'

Because repairing is a new behaviour for many people, particularly those who have been raised in wealthier families or away from older generations or in cities, ní Dhulchaointigh knew she would have to inspire people to mend; she would have to make it fun. 'It all started with a vision for a material that appeared magical,' she says.

Jane ní Dhulchaointigh, inventor and co-founder of Sugru

'I imagined a space-age rubber that could bond to anything, work in any environment and be super easy to use – as easy as Play-Doh. The aim in making it so versatile was to make it super useful, but also to trigger the imagination. Part of our role in the repair movement is to inspire people's first repair experience.' Early in the development process, she realised that silicone could fulfil that vision as well as being very durable, but the whole process from idea to launch took about six years including three years of invention and formulation. 'I worked with two retired silicone scientists who guided and trained me to do the lab work, until we could afford to hire students and then graduates to get the technology ready for market,' says ní Dhulchaointigh. 'At that pre-launch stage, there were thousands of experiments to achieve the magical combination of properties that enable Sugru to bond to so many different materials, not stick to your skin, go in the dishwasher, insulate against electricity – and all in a range of beautiful colours.'

The Sugru community has come up with thousands of pragmatic mends, fixing

A broken ceramic vase repaired in bright colours with Sugru

I imagined a space-age rubber that could bond to anything, work in any environment and be super easy to use.

everything from kettles and toasters to vacuum cleaners and mugs. It has protected beehives in Madagascar from rain, draughts and parasites. It has repaired bicycle tyres in Mongolia. And it has helped support a Lego toothbrush holder that a mum made for her kids.

Some of ní Dhulchaointigh's favourite applications are even more unusual. A customer in Ireland used Sugru to fashion a foot for a prosthetic leg for a chicken that had been injured in a fox attack. An anaesthetist working at a hospital in Haiti was able to get a better night's sleep, and therefore no doubt perform better in his work, after the tears in his mosquito net were patched with Sugru. 'When I was experimenting in the laboratory and building a production process, I often wondered how people would use this mouldable glue in their lives,' says ní Dhulchaointigh. 'I love the mosquito net fix because it's a really simple problem that would have been difficult to fix without Sugru, and it shows how a tiny, humble fix can make a huge difference.' David Constantine is a lifelong fixer, designer, inventor and photographer and also the founder of Motivation, a UK-based NGO. Having been paralysed by a diving accident in his youth, he uses Sugru to customise everyday objects such as remote controls, light switches, paintbrushes and cameras to make them easier to use. His most recent customisation prevented the oars on his boat from rotating, enabling him to get back on the water for the first time since his accident.

'When I started out enthusing about repair almost 20 years ago, a lot of people looked at me like I was crazy,' says ní Dhulchaointigh. 'Luckily, things are starting to shift and I really believe that someday we will look back on the "waste age" that we are living through now with horror and curiosity: "What were we thinking?!" "How did we live like that?" In the coming decades, new and different systems for living will emerge; systems that are truly nurturing of life – of people and the rest of the biosphere. We are thrilled to be part of the growing repair movement. We aim to inspire and feed into shifting the collective mindset and behaviour – using imagination to beat this throwaway society through community and millions of tiny little fixes. But I'm even more excited about the role that it can play in shifting our energies. Taking hands-on action in small and tangible ways can help build our energy to be part of the solution; it empowers us to think and feel differently; it triggers our imagination about living in more sustainable ways. Imagination is what will give us the leaps forward we are longing for.'

Sugru is highly durable, so it's often used to fix kitchen appliances
A zip-pull mended with Sugru extends the life of a suitcase

Sugru is flexible and electrically insulating, so phone-charging cables are the most popular item for repair

A tiny, humble fix can make a huge difference.

Vincent Dassi

‘Fixing objects is a way of taking ownership of them,’ says Vincent Dassi (1994, Tours, France). ‘It’s a way not just to make them functional again, but also to make them properly yours.’ The former woodworker and Design Academy Eindhoven graduate has developed a material and open-source methodology he calls Pulp It – a way of repairing almost anything using a paper pulp similar to papier-mâché, which can be moulded into three-dimensional forms and sets to an MDF-like consistency.

Deliberately low-tech and easy to make at home, Pulp It consists of paper clay – shredded cardboard mixed with water – and a glue made by combining rice flour with boiling water. Both can be mixed in a common household blender and then used to replace missing parts or repair broken

Vincent Dassi in his workshop

Preparation of the cardboard pulp

elements of everyday items, from chairs and vacuum cleaners to the precious guitar that inspired the project.

'The guitar was a very good quality one, but a friend gave it to me because it was too expensive to pay a guitar maker to fix,' he says. 'Since I had already used cardboard pulp and glue for making objects, I knew that it could be a solution for recreating the back of the guitar.'

Dassi blended cardboard with water to create a pulp, squeezed the excess water out with a self-made press, and then added natural glue to create a thick clay-like material that dries hard but remains porous, so that layers can be added over time – a process Dassi likens to 3D printing. 'I applied some clay, waited until it got hard and then added another layer – after a few days, it was possible to build back the whole missing part.' He attached the new back to the original guitar using wood glue. 'Something interesting about this material is that it is easy to add or take out a detail – and I managed to recreate a dense, natural material close to wood, with good sound quality too, even if it's a bit different from the original. I didn't just make the guitar functional again, I also made it properly mine, which gives a sentimental value to it.'

He realised his methodology could help people to prolong the lives of household goods and so posted the 'recipe' online (betterpulpit.com), along with videos demonstrating how to make everyday objects from scratch, such as a chair and a desk lamp (p. 34). 'I have tried to create a powerful tool that allows anyone to create and fix objects at home without needing power tools or a lot of money, and using locally sourced and sustainable materials,' he says. 'If you can fix things, you can also modify them and then become more independent,' he says. 'You do not need to buy a new object every time, and you also learn more about the way something works.'

Instead of preserving traditional repair techniques, he is offering new ones. 'I like to fix objects in a creative way, so that the function is restored, but we can also see that it's different,' he says. 'Fixing objects the way I do is not the "traditional way", which means that I am creating an alternative, which might displease some people, but it also offers opportunity to fix objects that would have been thrown away because of the prohibitive cost of repairing them. It's not for everyone, but to my mind, it is more authentic. Plus, people are usually curious about it – it starts conversations.' And those are conversations that need to be had. Dassi grew up in a home where mending and repair were commonplace. 'My dad was always fixing everything by himself at home – washing machines, cars, coffee machines... you name it,' he says. But that has changed, even in the three short decades since he was born. 'The overconsumption of objects around us is linked with the fact that we now replace more than we repair. Even something that is broken usually has a lot of perfectly working pieces, so buying a new object instead of fixing an old one leads to an overconsumption of resources that we might want to save in order to avoid climate change and pollution. Restoring objects is obviously a way to avoid waste.'

Dassi doesn't see himself as part of the repair movement. 'I am simply trying to do the best I can to create sustainable and accessible alternatives to throwing objects away,' he says. But he does want to see things change. 'Our way of consuming is not sustainable – I really hope that I will see in the coming years a paradigm shift in consumption, leading to a system not based on the constant pursuit of growth, but a more sober and humble way of living.'

I didn't just make the guitar functional again, I also made it properly mine.

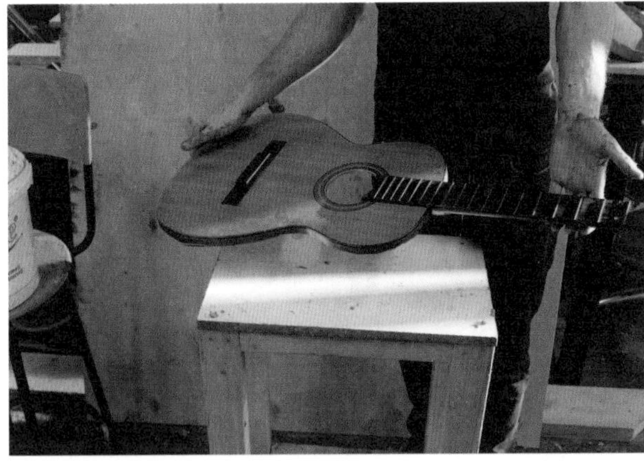
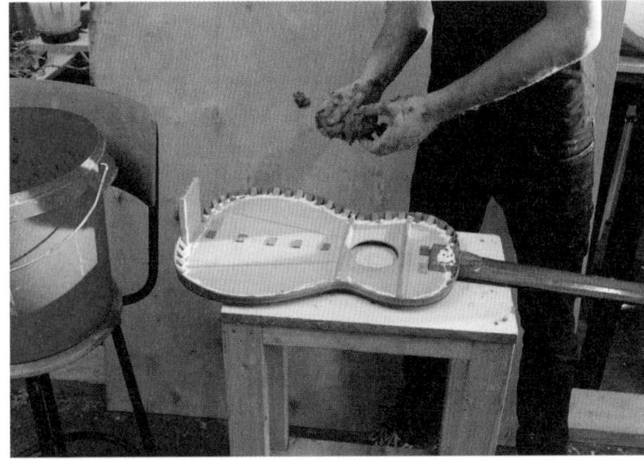

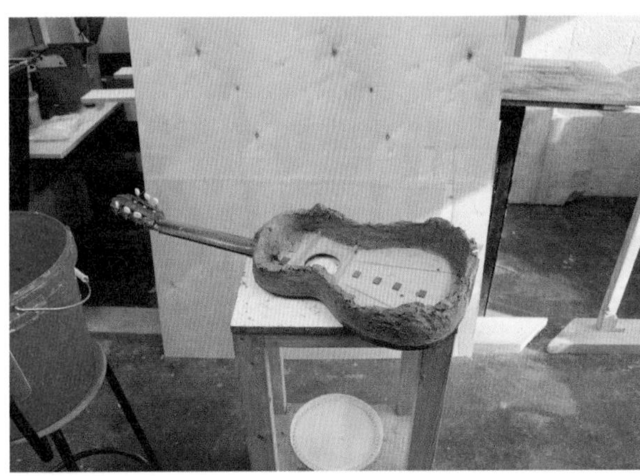

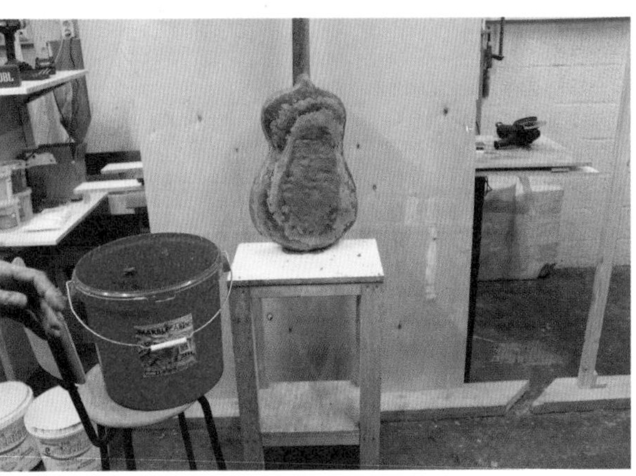

The process of repairing of a guitar. Every day, a layer of paper clay is added to the previous one, which has dried and hardened. Wood glue is used to connect the wood to the first layer of paper clay

Various objects made out of cardboard pulp

Fixing objects the way I do is not the ‘traditional way’, which might displease some people, but it also offers opportunity to fix objects that would have been thrown away.

Jude Dennis & Hannah Stanton

Former prop maker Jude Dennis (1973, Ponteland, UK) met former graphic designer Hannah Stanton (1974, Taunton, UK) while studying traditional and modern upholstery at the Cass, part of London Metropolitan University. With shared childhood experiences of rummaging through charity shops, an approach to DIY that Dennis describes as 'a little bit punk, a little bit bodger', and making and mending being the norm for both of them, they hit it off immediately. They were told that what they were learning was an artform in decline, but since they were just as interested in the 'modern' as the 'traditional' part of the course's title, they didn't buy that. 'Upholstery was spoken about as a heritage craft,' says Stanton. 'We started Second Sitters because we were told upholstery was dying, but that's not how we felt. In our eyes, it is very much a

Hannah Stanton (left) and Jude Dennis

Big Ball Balzac was Hannah Stanton's contribution to Second Sitters vs SCP, a live upholstery performance in London in 2017

Show Pony by Hannah Stanton

contemporary practice, and our work since then has been instrumental in bringing about change within the upholstery community. Fast forward 15 years, and there is definitely a resurgence – more training centres are opening, skills and techniques are evolving – and that's perhaps due to a different demographic. Upholsterers today are much more likely to be women, to use social media and to be community-based – it feels more dynamic now.'

Second Sitters is a not-for-profit creative partnership that the pair established in 2012, from a shared upholstery workshop in east London, to push the boundaries of what the 'modern' part of that course title might look like. As well as taking on private and commercial commissions separately, they work together to deliver publications, exhibitions, talks and collaborative working and education days to open up a conversation around what they describe as a 'hidden' craft. 'We are practising upholsterers, not afraid to question the status quo in order to keep the craft relevant and moving forward,' says Dennis. 'Our projects aim to be inclusive – to make connections with as wide an audience as possible and to provoke discussion, while providing a platform for expression and communication. Second Sitters is about more than the exhibitions, the zines, the happenings, the projects and the workshops – it's about creating a long-lasting community around upholstery.'

Second Sitters vs SCP was a live upholstery performance that took place at London's Geffrye Museum (now the Museum of the Home) in 2017 as part of Dennis and Stanton's touring exhibition, *Upholstery: Evolution to Revolution*. Furniture company SCP provided three Balzac chair frames – a modern take on a classic club chair designed by Matthew Hilton that appears in Taschen's *1000 Chairs*. Dennis, Stanton and Steve Allen, one of the in-house upholsterers at Coakley & Cox (SCP founder Sheridan Coakley's Norfolk-based upholstery manufacturer) – took one frame each. Allen upholstered the chair as it would usually be finished for SCP, while Dennis (pp. 42–43) and Stanton (above, left) subverted the traditional techniques and materials of upholstery to push the boundaries of the craft. Three strikingly different outcomes demonstrate the crucial role that upholstery plays in the final form of a chair.

Dennis's *Stackers* series (pp. 39–41) had a more prosaic starting point. 'I am drawn to chairs that have been abandoned, discarded or overlooked,' she says. 'I am an opportunist collector – that project came about because someone had dumped a stack of Robin Day Polyprop Chairs behind my workshop. I started upholstering them, restoring their function by elevating their status and putting them back into use. The chair that began the series, *Stacker 1*, was the first time Dennis attempted to use traditional upholstery techniques to repair a plastic chair. 'It was an experiment in how to attach traditional materials using traditional techniques to a contemporary frame,' she says. The chair has since been acquired for the Frederick Parker Collection – an educational resource spanning more than 300 years of British furniture making and design, from 1660 to the present day.

The Red Chair was another collaborative experiment with a live performance element – this time, a single chair was worked on across three consecutive days. Dennis took the back, Stanton the seat and Rachael South (p. 18) the arms. 'The chair came from a friend in the workshop – its original mid-century design is a classic shape,' says Dennis. 'By creating a radical change to its final appearance, we were better able to present the idea of an upholsterer as an independent thinker, designer and maker. Each person was given total freedom and the result mixed traditional materials and techniques with contemporary ideas and unexpected elements – an "exquisite corpse" of sorts.'

In Stanton's *Show Pony* (p. 37, right), the 'hidden craft' of traditional upholstery is laid bare. The horsehair fabric seat is traditionally sprung and stuffed, but Stanton exposed the usually concealed internal raw iron frame of a Victorian armchair as a hand-finished brass structure whose lines mirror the corsetry of the period. 'I was fascinated when I first encountered an iron-back chair,' she says. 'They were popular during the Victorian era when metal was a cheaper material than wood – the malleability of the metal allowed for curves and more intricate shapes to be formed. I wanted to expose the frame and its beauty but still have a functional piece.'

Their approach might be subversive and playful, but their message is serious. 'We use furniture as a medium for the exploration of ideas – engaging audiences to think differently about their furniture, what's in it, where it comes from and who has made it,' says Stanton. 'Reupholstery is saving something from landfill. Even if there's only an inkling of life left in a chair, it's worth saving – and there's a rush in giving something a new life. And, on a very basic level, materials can be reused in upholstery, even 100-year-old horsehair can be cleaned and re-carded.'

They are hopeful that the message is getting through to more and more people. 'Things are happening,' says Dennis. 'There is definitely a movement towards using more considered materials. And, as a living craft, the creative possibilities of upholstery, both conceptually and technically, are really starting to be explored. Now, it definitely feels like there is more of an understanding, a recognition of what upholstery is – upholsterers are even on TV!'

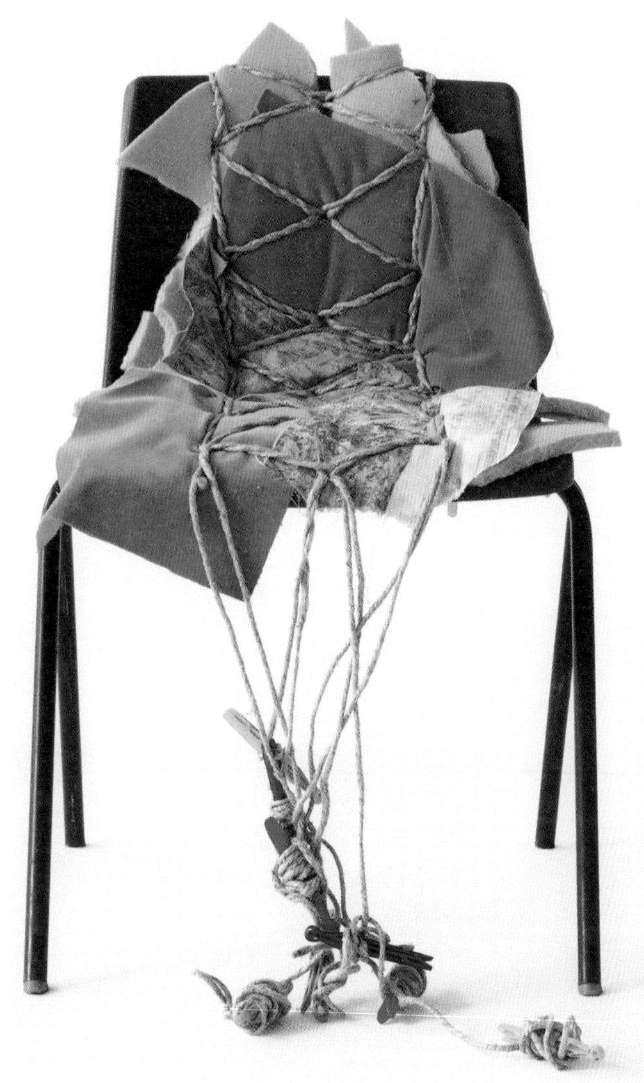

Bastard Beeralu Baby, from the *Stackers* series by Jude Dennis

BFF Bench, from the *Stackers* series by Jude Dennis (above and opposite)

We use furniture as a medium for the exploration of ideas – engaging audiences to think differently about their furniture, what's in it, where it comes from and who has made it.

Even if there's only an inkling of life left in a chair, it's worth saving – and there's a rush in giving something a new life.

Bastard Beeralu Balzac was Jude Dennis's contribution to Second Sitters vs SCP, a live upholstery performance in London in 2017 (right and opposite)

Chris Miller

Chris Miller (1975, Epsom, UK) was in Sri Lanka on 26 December 2004 when the tsunami hit the country's eastern and southern shores. 'Ordinarily, we made travel up as we went along, but on this occasion, we had booked various places in advance – and that's what saved our lives,' he says. Two days before, he and his then partner had reluctantly left the waterside hut they'd been staying in and moved inland to a pre-booked jungle lodge for Christmas Day. Within 48 hours, the tsunami had destroyed those waterside huts, taking the lives of many of the people with whom they'd been sharing drinks just days before. It was a wake-up call. 'We all experience signpost moments every day,' he says. 'Most we miss, some we see but don't act upon, and some hit us smack in the face.' Miller left his job in London and moved to Cornwall. Two years later, he launched

Chris Miller at the skinflint offices in Penryn, Cornwall

Product development engineer Rosy Seal tinkers with 1950s munitions store pendants in the skinflint workshop

vintage lighting brand skinflint – in response to an event made more likely and more severe by climate change. 'We simply can't go on in the way we have for the last 100 years,' he says. 'The resources are just not there.'

Miller credits his passion for restoration to his father, a jazz musician, and his mother, a teacher. Not only because theirs was a humble home where broken things were fixed, but because of the skills they endowed him with. 'The creativity my father gave me was balanced by my mother's empathy,' he says. 'And that sense of nurturing is an inherent part of mending and repair – you have to care.' That combination, together with his father's passion for antique shops and auctions, led to Miller's lifelong commitment to well-made vintage products that were built to last, but it was at art college where lighting got added into the mix. 'My first project was a lighting project, and lighting has been with me ever since,' he says. Miller went on to study product design at Sheffield Hallam University and ended up designing both lights and lighting schemes as a designer and consultant, but always felt that he was reinventing the wheel. It took that tragic personal experience in Sri Lanka to jolt him out of 'business as usual' and find his calling.

Skinflint specialises in sourcing lighting from the 1920s to the 1970s, usually from public and industrial buildings such as hospitals, churches and factories. The company has already saved 50,000 lights from landfill. The lights are made safe and compliant with modern regulations and then get what Miller calls a 'light touch' restoration, maintaining the patina of their age, before being sold to architects, interior designers and house-proud consumers the world over. 'If a light has got dinks and dunks in it, we won't try to patch those. We might remove rust or failing paint, but we would never add new paint,' he says. 'Then we lacquer them to freeze them in time.' The decision to source mainly industrial lights is about availability and volume, and his chosen era is bookended by the advent of mainstream electric lighting in the 1920s and the introduction of plastics in the 1970s. 'Buildings such as churches were the first to be electrified and we still salvage 1920s church lights, because they have had quite an easy life – they're only used once a week and they tend to be quite high up,' he explains. 'After the 1970s, you start to see the language of planned obsolescence and failure engineering coming into the documentation, and the effects of engineers handling a material they didn't yet fully understand.' Lights can be brought back to skinflint for repair if damaged, and a buy-back scheme (named 'Full Circle') allows customers to return lights they no longer need in exchange for credit to buy replacements.

Workshop assistant Pete Nichols polishing Czech glassware

We simply can't go on in the way we have for the last 100 years. The resources are just not there.

Despite selling to a global audience, Miller is keen to keep production local and employs both in-house staff at the skinflint offices and workshop in Penryn, Cornwall, and specialist restorers within a ten-kilometre radius. 'I'm really happy to sell to people all over the world, but with regards to the mechanics of the business, it's really important for me to keep that local,' he says. 'Despite being a popular tourist destination, Cornwall has some of the highest levels of poverty in Europe, so we want to put something back and even encourage people to relocate here. But there's also a sense that traditional restoration skills have been disrespected over recent decades, so we want to invest in those too. There's no way you could automate what our team do – every light is different and needs different interventions – and it is hard physical work, but there are a lot people who love the materials and the processes, and I like to think that what we do honours and respects that.'

It's clear that Miller wants to get every part of this business right – in 2021, skinflint became a B Corp, which he describes as 'a natural next step' – but coming back to that pivotal moment in Sri Lanka, it's doing something to fight the climate crisis specifically that gets him up in the morning. 'You can layer provenance and storytelling on top... but the key driver for our business is the environment,' he says. 'Look, I haven't got an S on my vest – I can't save the planet on my own, but I do what I can. If everyone did that, we might just be okay.'

Repair as storytelling

Repair [verb] – to restore something to a good condition, to renovate or mend by replacing or refixing parts or compensating loss or exhaustion, to remedy, to set right again[1]

Forget your perfect offering.
There is a crack in everything.
That's how the light gets in.

– Leonard Cohen, Anthem

'As good as new' is the phrase often uttered with pride after a successful fix. There is a sense of a returning to an original state in the word repair that can also be seen in the Latin *reparare* – to restore or to set back in order. But it's rarely as straightforward as this; any repair interrupts the narrative of an object, taking its story in a different direction. Whoever gets to decide the what, why, how and when of the repair also gets to dictate the rest of its story. The idea of a repair undoing or hiding damage is, in fact, a Western perspective; something Algerian-French artist Kader Attia describes as 'the myth of the perfect.' He explains:

> In Western society, the pinnacle of repair has been to erase all signs of the injury. [But] the word 'repair' is an oxymoron. Every repair is entangled with the injury – you cannot separate the two... In traditional societies, it's the opposite: they have ways to fix an injury that also keeps it visible... this [is the] difference between traditional and modern modes of repair: one that acknowledges the passing of time and the other one that aims to deny the effects of time.[2]

The relatively recent trend for 'visible mending' in the West often leans heavily on the traditional repair techniques that Attia mentions and, instead of hiding or 'burying the evidence' of damage or wear, reveals, exposes and even celebrates it – something Elizabeth Spelman describes as 'the creative destruction of brokenness'.[3]

To contemporary Westerners, perhaps the most well-known example of visible repair is *kintsugi*. The Japanese technique dates back to the late 16th or early 17th century and involves repairing broken ceramics using fine *urushi* lacquer and powdered gold (or silver in the case of *gintsuki*) to both rejoin and highlight the cracks. It is a highly pragmatic technique enabling the vessels to retain their former functionality, but one that also tells a story. Bonnie Kemske, former editor of *Ceramic Review* and author of *Kintsugi: The Poetic Mend*, describes *kintsugi* as 'an intimate metaphoric narrative of loss and recovery, breakage and restoration, tragedy and the ability to overcome it'.[4] The stories embodied in a *kintsugi*-repaired vessel make it more valuable than something 'as good as new' and remind us that there is life after – and alongside – injury.

Kintsugi is far from the only historical example of 'repair entangled with injury' – of repair as storytelling. In Brazil, *gambiarra* is a bricolage – or what Richard Sennett calls a 'dynamic repair'[5] – technique in which objects or materials are hacked to perform new functions, offering a way to avoid the imported aesthetic that comes with mass production and globalisation,[6] and instead create something uniquely Brazilian. *Gambiarra* has parallels all over the world and similar practices can be found in China, Kenya and India. The Chinese call their approach *zizhu chuangxin*; the Kenyans, *jua kali*; and in India it is *jugaard* (also spelled *juugard* and *jugaad*). 'Jugaard is about finding solutions to problems by taking a non-linear and innovative approach,' says textile designer Kangan Arora. 'It is a state of mind that rejects wastage and assumes everything is repairable by making materials and tools perform far beyond their intended use.' *Kantha* (also *katha*, *kheta* and *gudri*) is another practice of remaking, originating in Bangladesh and the Indian states of West Bengal, Tripura and Odisha. The practice involves the reuse of fabric, usually saris, layered and connected with a distinctive running stitch, trapping air for warmth, and creating symbolic iconography, which infuses the final piece with narrative. 'The tradition of *kantha* is rooted in thrift, but there is a very strong undercurrent of making something emotional,' says textile artist Ekta Kaul (p. 144). 'When mothers, grandmothers and aunties make a *kantha* blanket from their own saris for a new baby, the idea of surrounding the baby with love is intrinsic.'

However, in contrast with *kintsugi*, which due to the cost of both the materials used and the skill required, tended to be reserved for important and valuable objects, what these practices have in common is the combination of ingenuity and scarce resources to reach improvised solutions.[7] The acknowledgement of the passing of time to which Attia refers often has a complex relationship with the material lack that drove their emergence.

Although there is a tradition of patchwork in Europe and North America, European darns were traditionally invisible. The British Government-led Make Do & Mend initiative attempted to popularise visible mending during the Second World War. In 1941, an issue of *Women's Magazine* proclaimed that 'patches, once a sign of poverty, are now a sign of patriotism'.[8] However, contrary to popular belief and despite the government's best efforts, repair continued to mean very different things to different people. For already skilled working-class women, mending had been necessary long before the war and continued to be afterwards. Despite the confident claims of *Women's Magazine*, for these women, patches and darns remained a sign of poverty and were kept hidden: 'I don't think it's right to look shabby in wartime. It lowers morale,' a working-class woman wrote in her diary.

So, who exactly was sporting these 'patriotic patches' during the war? For middle- and upper-class women, unused to mending and with time on their hands, and for servicemen who were issued with a mending kit called a 'hussif' ('housewife')[9] while they were away from their wives and mothers, mending was something of a novelty. At the height of Make Do & Mend in 1942, not a single issue of *Vogue* mentions darning; instead, articles advise readers to 're-fashion for Spring'.[10] Meanwhile, titles aimed at working-class women such as *Woman's Magazine* offered advice on how to fix a skirt that 'showed bad signs of wear'.[11] And despite servicemen darning their own socks, the Women's Institute reported that 'sock mending seems to be our chief military occupation today' with 5,853 groups across the country undertaking the work.[12]

Rationing was intended to ensure fairness, but Make Do & Mend relied upon the garments that people already owned, which were far from equally distributed. As one upper-middle-class woman commented in her diary: 'I'm so well stocked that if the war lasted 20 years, I'd be all right.'[13] There was a definite sense of servicemen and middle- and upper-class women 'playing at' repair. The fact that the slang term 'make and mend' for an afternoon off is still used in the British Royal Navy[14] reinforces the association between mending and leisure for these groups. A practice that was a source of shame for some groups became a source of fun for others.

Those for whom mending was a necessity then see it as something to be hidden to this day. My aunt, who lived through Make Do & Mend, reserves repaired clothes for housework and gardening. I asked her how she would feel about wearing them outside the house: 'It would make me feel cheaper and less worthy,' she said. 'Seeing someone else in darned clothes would make me feel sorry for them, because they would seem so poor as not to be able to have nice clothes.'

While middle- and upper-class women and servicemen appropriated repair techniques from working-class women, many of the techniques popularised by the contemporary visible mending trend have been appropriated from traditional cultures and societies. More than 158,000 Instagram posts are currently tagged with #visiblemending,[15] showing that plenty of people do wear repaired clothes as badges of honour today – as narrative devices that enable them to reclaim and subvert traditional notions of 'women's work' while taking a stance against the human and environmental cost of fast fashion and the capitalist system that has fuelled its growth.

One of the most popular techniques in the contemporary visible mending movement – popularised by how-to books such as Katrina Rodabaugh's *Mending Matters*[16] and Kerstin Neumüller's *Mend & Patch*[17] – is the application of white running stitch, either in parallel or intersecting lines forming tiny crosses, to patched denim. The patched denim is a sanitised version of *boro*, while the white running stitch is inspired by *sashiko*, two techniques that emerged in 19th-century Japan.

What is the problem with one group appropriating the skills of another and making them visible? Pierre Bourdieu was a French sociologist who coined the term 'cultural capital' through his research into power dynamics and the ways in which power and influence are conferred through generations to maintain social order. Among his findings is the idea that the value of cultural capital is at least partly dependent upon social recognition[18] – and therefore visibility – and the notion that a practice is transformed when someone takes it across class barriers and its associated identity 'ceases to be what it is as soon as he appropriates it'.[19] Science and technology historian Steven Jackson argues that the freedom to choose to show or hide parts of ourselves and our stories is linked to power and privilege.[20] Appropriation happens when members of a dominant group take something from a subjugated group, and benefit from it in a way the group who originated it cannot. *Boro* and *sashiko* provide the perfect example of this.

The two techniques evolved together in the 19th century as resource-poor Japanese families acquired scraps of cotton from sailors visiting the north of Japan from the more prosperous south, from rag salesmen,[21] or even – in the case of Buddhist monks – from the street, cremation sites or prior use as 'excrement wiping cloths'.[22] *Sashiko* (literally 'little stabs') stitches were used to fill gaps, patch holes and layer fabrics into a single bolt of *boro* – a retrospectively coined term for the resulting warm, durable, quilted and patchworked fabric, meaning 'tattered' or 'repaired'.[23] In a society in which there were strict rules about what each caste could wear, the indigo of the *boro* denoted physical labour[24] and white *sashiko* stitching represented 'nothing more than the resourcefulness necessary to survive'.[25] As alternatives became available, the *boro* garments and *sashiko* stitching skills that were once passed down from mother to daughter became 'a haunting testament to the poverty-stricken past'[26] that many would rather forget – if only they could be allowed to.

As art collectors began to see the aesthetic value of *boro*, they started to acquire not only garments, but the stories that went with them – stories that the people from whom they obtained the *boro* were reluctant to share. Japanese clothing expert Tatsuichi Horikiri, who owns 3,500 'specimens' (which can fetch tens of thousands of pounds at auction), recounts several such exchanges:

> 'I begged and begged until reluctantly, she finally started to tell the story.'
>
> 'The shop owner… felt it morally wrong to expose the [*boro*] to the curious eyes of casual viewers… after long negotiations, I finally succeeding in obtaining it, but the owner refused to accept any payment.'[27]

Horikiri speaks about his collection with reverence, rejecting the term *boro* and describing the *kokoro* (variously translated in his books as 'heart', 'emotions' and 'feelings'[28]) stitched into the garments as 'trying to tell us their stories'. These are stories that involve abject poverty – fishermen's *boro* coats that did not have time to dry between one day's work and the next, and mothers who did not have enough *boro* nappies to change them when they became soiled[29] – and they have often been reluctantly relinquished in return for little or no payment, begging the question, who has the right to ask about, hear and retell these stories? Art collectors monetising, decontextualising and making visible such memories feels deeply problematic, but once again shows that while the system is broken for some, it is working just fine for others. The commodification and fetishisation of these techniques as 'inspiration' for white Western visible menders, who haven't taken the time to hear these stories before using words like 'boro' and 'sashiko' to tell their own story, is perhaps equally problematic.

Visible mending in the Global North is no longer driven by functional need; it is driven by the existential necessity of responding to very urgent human rights and environmental crises. However, there is a delicate balance to be struck between learning from cultures such as those in Japan that value the patina of age, and aping and co-opting practices in such a way as to constitute harmful appropriations of culture and/or class. When repair becomes an act of storytelling, it is important that we respect the history of both object and technique, and make sure that the stories we are sharing are ours to tell.

The curators, menders and remakers profiled in this chapter all strike that balance deftly – respecting not only the narratives of the objects they repair, but also of the techniques they use to do so. British textile artist Celia Pym (p. 54) draws on her own European heritage of darning to make visible the repairs she makes to clothes, learning their stories in order to be of service to their owners. 'I am interested in the holes,' she says. 'Damage gives clues to not only the life of the garment but the actions, movements and experiences of the owner.' Dutch conservator-turned-artist Bouke de Vries (p. 62) takes the notion of keeping the injury visible to its zenith and places the broken pieces of a vase in a glass replica of its original form, whereas Raewyn Harrison (p. 76) builds missing Delftware pots to house the broken shards that remain of them. The exhibition *R for Repair* curated by Hans Tan (p. 86) explored contemporary mending in a Singaporean design context, where few of the designers he commissioned have any family memories of repair. And Keiko Matsui (p. 68) is exploring *yobitsugi* – an extension of *kintsugi* – to explore her Japanese identity within the cultural context of her new home in Australia.

Celia Pym

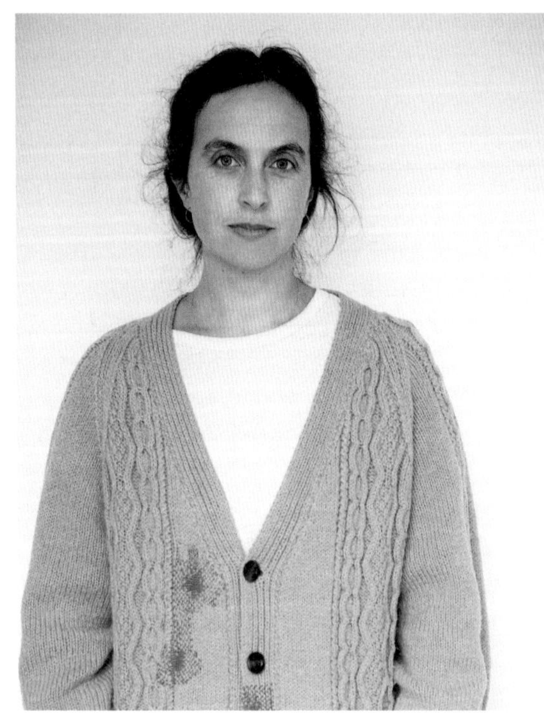

Celia Pym

You often need to read the wall text to understand what an object in a museum is trying to say, but when artist and self-described 'expert in holes' Celia Pym (1978, London, UK) darned a paper bag for the Design Museum's 2021–2022 *Waste Age* exhibition, its story was immediately clear. The seeming contradiction between the care imbued into her intersecting, colourful stitches and something as ephemeral as a brown paper potato sack seemed jarring at first – and then suddenly brilliant. It asked, 'What is worth mending?'

'I opened a paper bag of potatoes one day and it tore down the side,' says Pym. 'Looking at the tear, I wondered what it would feel like mended back together.' She had already been experimenting with darning newspapers, inspired by the late American artist Ed

Rossbach's use of found materials and his woven newspaper baskets, and she liked the feel of wool and paper together. 'Soft and smooth – and when you puncture paper, that's the hole you've got – you can't take it back,' she says. 'I mended the paper bag I'd torn using wool [p. 58]. As always, letting the damage lead – just following the tear. A stitched scar up the side.'

Pym grew up in a family of makers and menders and had a childhood filled with imaginative play. 'We made a lot of things out of paper and glue, dressed up in sheets, and built stuff out of cushions,' she recalls, describing her parents, aunts and uncles as 'creative role models: good gardeners, cooks, knitters, and menders and fixers'. She cites her great-aunt Elizabeth, 'a mender and a fixer', and her grandmother, who 'enjoyed fashion, colour, pattern and cloth', as particular influences. But it was the death of her great-uncle Roly – and one jumper in particular – that sparked her interest in darning.

'We were clearing out his things and my dad gave me a mended jumper that had belonged to him,' she says. 'I was really moved by the darning I could see in it. These very pragmatic mends had been made by my great-aunt Elizabeth. I was touched by these small, practical acts of care, and I loved how the damage exactly paired up with the particular movements of my uncle's body, how it embodied him and his actions. Right up until the end of his life, he would draw – a wooden board resting across the arms of his chair – and you could see where his jumper had become threadbare on his lower arms as they moved across that board.'

Elizabeth died before Roly and Pym was sad to see the newest holes remained undarned, so she decided to undertake one last act of care for him. The problem was, she didn't know how. Undeterred, she took herself off to the library and looked up 'darning' in Thérèse de Dillmont's *Encyclopedia of Needlework*. This was in 2007 and if the trend for 'visible mending' was already happening, Pym wasn't aware of it. She did, however, want to differentiate her beginner darns from her great-aunt's practised hand. Elizabeth had mended her brother's jumper with whatever yarn she had to hand, so the colour matches weren't always accurate, but they were 'whiteish' – Pym chose blue. 'I continue to use contrasting colours to mend with because I want to see what is missing – in some ways, I am more interested in the damage than the repair.'

In 2017, Pym entered the Woman's Hour Craft Prize with mended items that belonged to people who worked in healthcare – an act of care for those who care professionally. By this point, Pym – a former nurse and qualified teacher – was a fully fledged artist working from a bright studio in her Victorian home in London, with big windows, textile-filled plastic tubs stacked floor to ceiling, and corkboards layered with images and ideas. She had visited Bill, a retired GP, having asked if he had anything in need of repair. After a long conversation about anything but, he finally produced an orange tank top knitted for him by his late wife Ursie. He told Pym how Ursie knew the size and shape of his body so well that she could knit without measurements. The sweater-vest had become moth-eaten and he was embarrassed to have let that happen. Pym repaired it with a yellow yarn of his choosing, and *Bill's Sweater* became one of the pieces shortlisted for the prize and displayed at London's Victoria & Albert Museum. Afterwards, it was returned to Bill, who wore it with pride untill he passed away in 2021.

Celia Pym in her studio

In some ways, I am more interested in the damage than the repair.

As part of the V&A exhibition, Pym was invited to host a series of mending events. She held an open call, inviting people to bring garments with holes in for her to darn. In previous workshops, she had started to notice patterns of damage and repair. This time, she decided to document them. 'I had a brand-new black tracksuit, socks, gloves and hat laid out like a body,' she says. 'For each holey item brought in, either I or the owner of the item would cut a corresponding hole in the tracksuit body and then I would darn it in the same colour we had chosen to mend the 'real' item. In this way, I was mapping out the damage brought in over the course of the event. All the mended items were returned to their owners, and I was left with *Where Holes Happen* [p. 61] – a map of all the mends.'

The map not only recorded the damage and subsequent repair, but the story behind each hole. 'My mending stations become consultation desks and, when I ask about damage, people tell me about their lives,' says Pym. 'Understanding the story behind an object changes its value; makes you appreciate it differently. The increased visibility of mended items is shifting values about what we want to keep, look after and care for – and not just objects, but people and the environment too. Stories deepen your feelings towards, and understanding of, things you might not have directly experienced, but they stay in your imagination in a powerful way.'

In his book, *The Day the World Stop Shopping*, JB MacKinnon argues that the first symbol of a world that consumes less might not be 'a charming tote store bag that has replaced our plastic bags, but a plastic bag that has been patched so it can last a little longer.'[1] The soft creases of paper, plastic or cloth, a jumble of irregular hand stitches, and the stories stitched into the damage might just represent the worn, weathered aesthetic of care and repair we all need to embrace.

1 JB MacKinnon, *The Day the World Stops Shopping* (London: Penguin Random House, 2021), 153.

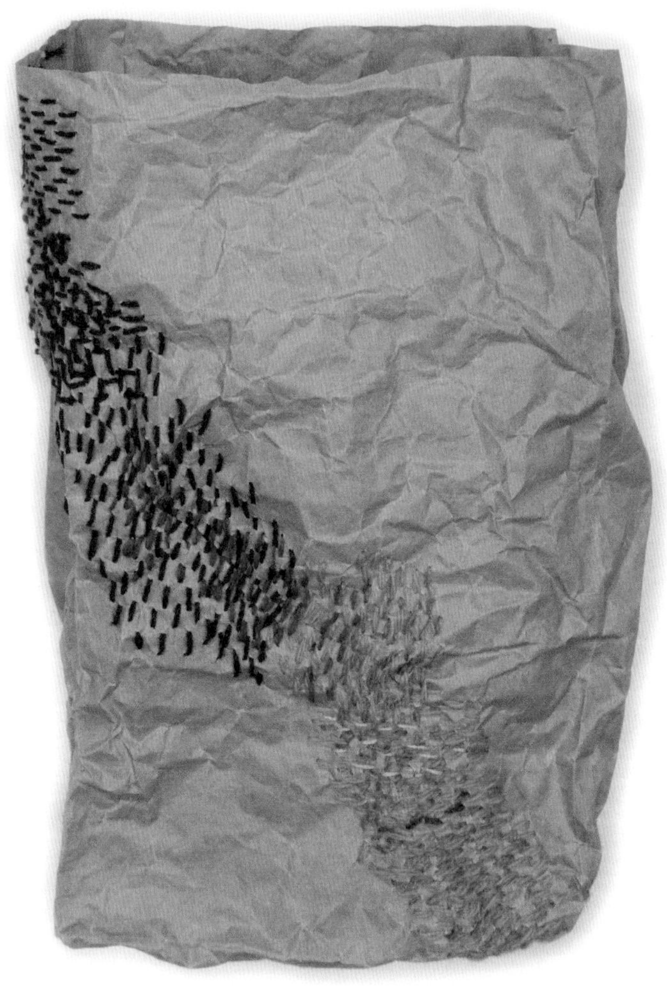

Mended Potato Bag, 2020. Paper bag and wool

When you puncture paper, that's the hole you've got – you can't take it back.

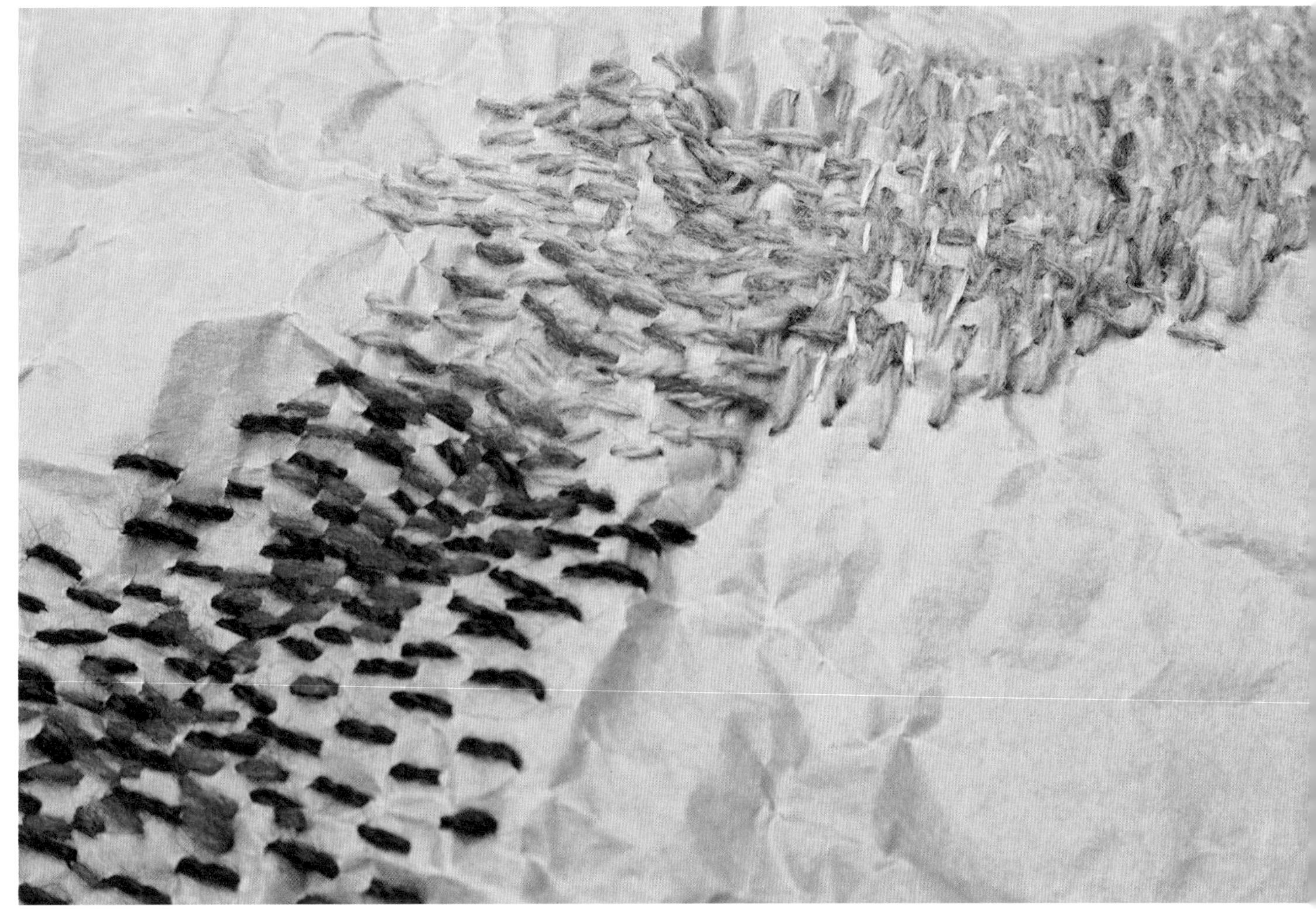

Detail of *Mended Potato Bag*, 2020. Paper bag and wool

Where Holes Happen in progress

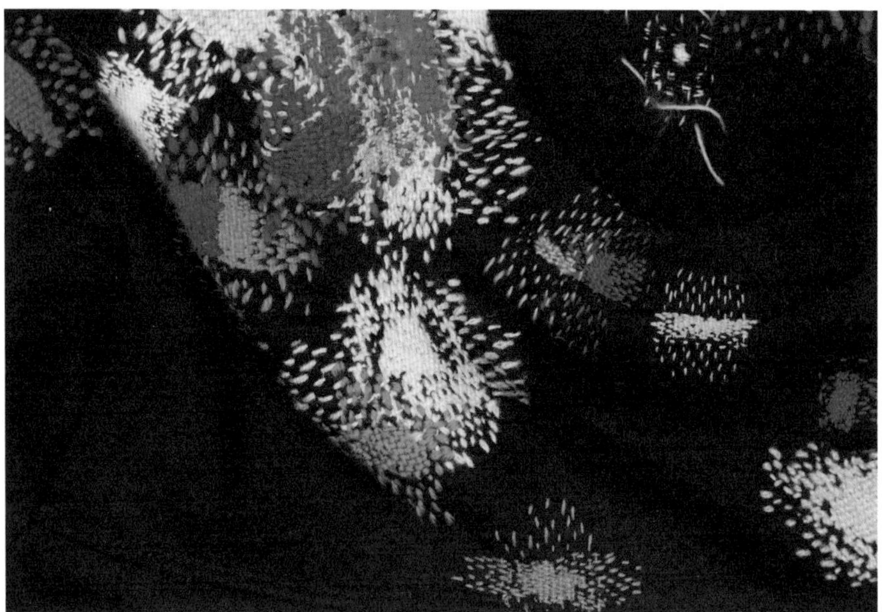

Detail of *Where Holes Happen*

Where Holes Happen, 2018. Tracksuit, sports socks, gloves, hat and various yarns

Bouke de Vries

In the *Memory Vessels* series (pp. 66–67) by London-based artist Bouke de Vries (1960, Utrecht, Netherlands), it isn't the object that gets repaired as much as the idea of the object. He takes shards of broken ceramics dating from anywhere between the 17th and 19th centuries and carefully reconstructs them to work out their original proportions. The range is wide: Asian, European and Delft; pottery, porcelain and earthenware; urns, ginger jars, pitchers and vases. He then commissions a precise replica in glass and displays the broken pieces inside. In his *Tobacco Jar Garniture* (opposite), three jars demonstrate different approaches – one is repaired with gold lacquer using the Japanese technique of *kintsugi*; one has the broken pieces mounted on brass pins, mimicking the effect of an explosion; and the pieces of the final jar are contained in a glass replica reminiscent of his *Memory Vessels* series. These sculptural pieces are thus both whole and broken, repaired and damaged and, crucially, tell the story of what de Vries describes as 'the most dramatic episode' in the original vessel's life.

De Vries has worked in fashion and studied at Design Academy Eindhoven and Central Saint Martins in London, but it was a long career as a conservator that finally inspired him to become an artist. 'There was only one restoration course in the Netherlands and it ran on a four-year cycle,' he says. 'I'd just missed it, so rather than waiting for three years, I applied to art schools instead, but I didn't have a portfolio. Luckily, Design Academy Eindhoven didn't want one – they chose students based on a day of tests and exercises, and I got in.' An internship in London led to him switch courses to Central Saint Martins followed by a six-year career in fashion – but he hated it. His partner suggested he returned to his first love of restoration and he found a course at West Dean College in Sussex. De Vries chose ceramics, and suddenly his textile design skills came to the fore. 'It turns out that decorating ceramics is quite similar to textile design – and there were people on that course who had never even held a paintbrush,' he laughs. 'That, combined with the fact that we had three hot meals a day and en-suite accommodation in the middle of a recession, and it was my second chance to study, meant that I felt very lucky to be there and just worked the whole time. I absolutely loved it.'

He started working as a glass and ceramics restorer as soon as he graduated. He's had a successful 15-year career working on pieces from the prehistoric to the contemporary, attracting high-profile clients such as the Victoria & Albert Museum and Grayson Perry, but he found himself missing the creativity he had enjoyed at college. 'When I'm restoring, I have to put my creativity to one side and make whole what somebody else has created,' he says. 'You can't think "Oh, that leaf would look much nicer if I gave it a little swirl" – you have to stick to the original.' That resulted in what he describes as an 'unfulfilled gap in my being' and he began to think about what sort of art he might make for himself. 'I thought, "work with what you know". And I know restoration, so I decided to take broken things as my starting point.'

Tobacco Jar Garniture, 2020. 18th-century Dutch Delft tobacco jars and mixed media

Horrified by the drop in value that a simple hairline crack could inflict on precious ceramic pieces – sometimes to the extent that they wouldn't warrant the cost of restoration – and curious about how repairs were often made invisible to the untrained eye, he started to explore a different approach to his craft, one that celebrated the history of each piece. As part of an internship at the V&A, he was invited to restore a glass Roman funeral urn designed to hold the ashes of the dead, and the seed for what was to become the *Memory Vessels* was planted.

Two turning points took the art element of his practice from a side hustle to his main focus (he still does some restoration work). One was getting a call from curator and collector Kay Saatchi, who nominated his work for an exhibition at Selfridges in 2009 highlighting 'rising stars' of the art world. 'His work is about things in decay,' she said in her nomination.

The second happened more recently, when pictures of his *Memory Vessels* series went viral during the Covid pandemic 'People were sharing the images, saying "This is how I'm feeling",' says de Vries. 'Somebody even changed the name and for a while one image was doing the rounds under the title "In Pieces but Holding It Together".' De Vries is conscious that although the breakages he highlights might represent the most dramatic moment in a vessel's life, they are far from the only stories it holds – they are often simply the only ones we know about. In the same way, the stories he intends to tell aren't always the ones that people read into his work. 'But I think it's great, because it's doing its job – it's making people think.'

When I'm restoring, I have to put my creativity to one side and make whole what somebody else has created.

Bouke de Vries

Memory Vessel 35, 2015. 16th-century Chinese Wan-Li porcelain jar, cover and glass

Memory Vessel 46, 2016. 17th-century Chinese Kang-Xi famille verte porcelain, glass and gold leaf

Memory Vessel 43, 2016. 18th-century Chinese Qing dynasty famille rose porcelain and glass

Keiko Matsui

Keiko Matsui

Keiko Matsui (1969, Osaka, Japan) grew up surrounded by handcrafted and carefully designed objects. 'Although we lived in an ordinary household, there was *ikebana* [an intentional flower arrangement used to adorn the *tokonoma*, or alcove, of a traditional Japanese home] with beautiful ceramic vases and calligraphy scrolls on the wall next to a house-shrine for our ancestors,' she says. 'In contrast to these traditional cultural objects, there was also Western-style furniture, lamps, and quirky stuffed toys of Japanese cartoon characters. Our house was always full of objects, some could be considered junk, and some held meaningful memories and stories. Growing up in Japan, where crafts are highly regarded and there is no distinguishable border between art and craft, my eye for observing objects became naturally more sophisticated over the years.'

The process of *kintsugi* – applying the gold powder

Having hand-sewn kimonos with her grandmother from the age of 12, Matsui was soon making her own clothes. Attending one of the few high schools in Osaka that didn't require a uniform gave her plenty of opportunity to experiment – she even made her own graduation gown, inspired by the Italian fashion designer Romeo Gigli. She says that at least half the clothing she wears to this day is made or repaired by her own hand.

Despite this immersion in craft and design throughout her childhood and teens, and a natural aptitude for making, it was only after travelling solo around the world in her early twenties and ending up in Australia that she decided to study ceramics at the National Art School in Sydney. It wasn't until she'd completed her degree that she sought out *kintsugi*, the technique that now informs much of her work. 'My porcelain *Scar Vessels* explored the altering and reforming of fine porcelain forms through the cutting and rejoining of sections,' she says. 'I would leave the joint seam line visible to juxtapose a finely thrown surface with the distressed joint. *Kintsugi* celebrates the damage and subsequent visible mending that results from the use of important functional objects. I realised that this philosophy was the same concept as my *Scar Vessels*.' Having made the connection, she sought out a master craftsperson in Japan to learn *kintsugi* – not so much with the intention of learning how to repair broken pottery, but in order to better understand how its process echoes her own ceramic practice.

Today, Matsui lives in Melbourne, which she describes as 'the most creative city in Australia' and works from a studio in a small, mud-brick cottage next to a weeping mulberry tree at Montsalvat in Eltham. 'Montsalvat was established in 1934 and is Australia's oldest artists' colony,' she explains. 'I appreciate every moment that I can practise my art at this historically rich and environmentally abundant space.' It is from this studio, surrounded by wild roses, peacocks, ducks and geese, that she now repairs broken ceramics for customers using both natural *urushi* tree-sap lacquer (sourced from Kyoto) and epoxy glue for the *kintsugi* repairs, which are finished with whichever material best suits the customer's needs for their object. 'When you open my studio door, you are met by my collection of *kintsugi*-repaired blue and white ceramic plates hanging on the wall,' she says.

But there's more to her work than traditional *kintsugi*. 'I am currently challenging myself to create contemporary ceramic-based objects that embed the philosophy of *kintsugi* – I am researching the potential of *kintsugi* beyond the technical scope of repair,' she says. 'In other words, I am creating new bodies of work that evoke distress, displacement and care, incorporating irregular, accidental or distressed lines of broken objects as a reference point. I am embedding the philosophy of *kintsugi* in my work, which embraces damage and imperfection as beauty. As such, I cut, tear, throw, imprint, stretch, deform, deconstruct and reconstruct. Through these techniques, I am exploring the possibility of a methodology within the materiality of clay, evoking a poetic, metaphoric notion of *kintsugi*.' Part of this project is to revisit her *Scar Vessels*, evolving them into a new body of work. 'I want to recall the time of creation of the *Scar Vessels* and reflect on my feelings when I was making them,' she says. 'This project is not actual repair, yet suggests *kintsugi* as a metaphoric language within the process of making.'

Matsui in her studio, Montsalvat, Melbourne

Kintsugi display in the studio

People will not repair a broken object if it is not personal, valuable or historical... it must have a story, a connection to the heart, in some way.

As well as *kintsugi*, Matsui also explores *yobitsugi* – replacing missing fragments with pieces from other ceramics to complete the restoration – which emerged as an extension of *kintsugi* repair. 'I am attempting to incorporate old shards of blue and white Japanese porcelain, in a way that integrates my identity with the cultural connection to my new home in Australia,' she says. 'Many people are influenced and impacted by globalisation, and the concept behind the artwork seems to resonate with many immigrants.'

Kintsugi has only recently become well known in Australia, and Matsui believes she is one of a handful of artists who introduced the practice to the community. 'People will not repair a broken object if it is not personal, valuable or historical,' she says. 'Therefore, it must have a story, a connection to the heart, in some way. Their relationship to the object is strong enough for them to want to find a way to keep it. Repair is an artistic and poetic way to do that. We live in a fast-moving, consumer-driven society, where more is more. By choosing mending and repair, and the stories that accompany each object, we are bringing attention to this problem. We are choosing to slow down, take time and value objects for more than their function. For me, the stories become ones about appreciating what we have now and learning to be more present with, and appreciative of, what we have.'

Describing herself as both a dreamer and a realist, Matsui says she hopes and dreams of a better world but also sees how power, money and authority disrupt people's lives every day. 'However, the small steps taken by each one of us may change the world for the better,' she says. 'If we understand the process of making, including the hours of labour behind the products we purchase, we may appreciate it more and start keeping fewer, better objects in our everyday lives. This is my hope.'

I am creating new bodies of work that evoke distress, displacement and care, incorporating irregular, accidental or distressed lines of broken objects as a reference point.

Matsui repairing a customer's Japanese vase

I am attempting to incorporate old shards of blue and white Japanese porcelain, in a way that integrates my identity with the cultural connection to my new home in Australia.

Matsui's new project using old shards of blue and white porcelain

Matsui's *kintsugi* tools and materials

Raewyn Harrison

'Someone once told me that holding one of my pieces in their hands was like holding a little bit of history,' says London-based ceramic artist Raewyn Harrison (1964, Wellington, New Zealand), a 'mudlark' who scours the foreshore of the River Thames for discarded clay pipes, handmade pins, old glass, bricks and shards of 16th-century Delftware to incorporate into her work.

The term mudlark was coined in the late 18th century to describe someone who scavenges for anything of value (often coal that had fallen off barges) in the mud that becomes exposed at low tide. Today's mudlarks are looking for objects – or, more often, fragments of objects – from the past that provide clues about how Londoners used to live. You need a permit from the Port of London Authority to remove items from the Thames foreshore and significant finds must be reported to the Museum of London. Trapped in the anaerobic mud, the treasures Harrison is looking for have been protected for centuries – the lack of exposure to air preserving them – and are surprisingly plentiful: clay pipes were once thrown away like cigarette butts.

Once she has collected these 'fragments from other people's lives', she sets about creating a new life for them. She inserts Delftware fragments into plain white porcelain tea bowls that she hand-throws, using *yobitsugi*. Typically, a new piece is inserted into an existing object or pieces of broken vessels are patched together to create new work. 'In my case it's a found object that I insert into something I have made,' she says. 'I make Delft tea bowls to

Raewyn Harrison at her studio in Lloyd Park, London

tell the story of the London Delft workers in the 16th century. I will cut a hole in my hand-thrown tea bowl to house a small fragment of pottery that I have found in the mud – I like taking a discarded object and elevating its status by using porcelain.'

Alongside the tea bowls, she also throws porcelain bottles to house fragmented glass bottlenecks, carefully calculating how much each piece will shrink when it is fired in the kiln to ensure the neck of the porcelain bottle ends up the right size for the glass neck to fit into. If she doesn't insert a fragment, she might press its texture into the surface of the clay or photograph it to make a ceramic transfer for one of her bowls or remnants of clay pipes. 'Most of the objects I collect are rubbish from centuries ago, but I value them for the insight they give about how Londoners lived,' she says. 'The River Thames is an endless source of inspiration – a potter's thumb print, the brush stroke on a bit of Delftware or the transfer image of the Willow pattern made famous in Stoke-on-Trent are all treasures that inform my making.' She uses porcelain because its white colour provides a good blank canvas for the stories she wants to share, and its dense plasticity makes it perfect for taking impressions.

Harrison grew up by the sea in New Zealand, playing with flotsam and jetsam collected from the beach, then travelled to London and stayed to study architecture. She became fascinated by the layers of history she discovered doing site-specific research. 'Once I realised that you could learn about London through the objects you can collect from the Thames, I became hooked on visits

Once I realised that you could learn about London through the objects you can collect from the Thames, I became hooked on visits to the river.

to the river,' she says. 'The objects I collect from its muddy shores have sometimes been sitting there from the moment they were lost or thrown away. Materials left over from previous industry along the river tell us a lot about the type of activity that took place there.'

From her studio in Walthamstow's Lloyd Park – also home to the William Morris Gallery – she researches maps to connect these tales together. 'My storytelling is quite site-specific because of the objects I find and where I find them,' she says. 'I delve into the archives and discover so much detail of what life was like from old maps and panoramas – they provide a context to my finds and bring my pieces alive. As human beings, it's important to connect to our past to inform where we go in the future. The Thames is a history of what we do with rubbish – by exploring what has been left behind we can see what has had a negative impact on the environment.'

Harrison not only tells these stories through her own work, she has also collaborated with Thames archaeologist Mike Webber and fellow mudlark and author of *Mudlarking*

Cargo, 2016. Slip-cast porcelain boxes containing various glazes in response to finds from the Thames foreshore

Lara Maiklem, to create public engagement artworks and exhibitions. 'By understanding what has been dumped in the Thames estuary throughout history, we can see the impact of industrialisation and recognise that we need to make sure regulations are robust enough to protect the environment,' she says. 'Nature can reclaim and create new habitats on the river. The RSPB [Royal Society for the Protection of Birds] has one of the largest designated areas in the country for birds at Cliffe Pools in the Thames estuary and it's a reminder of what can be done when we stop polluting our rivers.' By telling the stories of what our ancestors threw away, Harrison is asking us to be mindful of the things we buy, make, keep, mend and discard ourselves. 'The rubbish sites at Tilbury and Mucking are a lesson in modern waste – plastics and polyester fabrics are now revealed in layers along the river's eroding banks,' she says. Somehow it seems unlikely that the mudlarks of the future will be as delighted with those finds as she is with a shard of Delftware.

Some of Harrison's favourite tools and textures are from the Thames foreshore

As human beings, it's important to connect to our past to inform where we go in the future. The Thames is a history of what we do with rubbish.

Treasures from the Thames, 2020. Slip-cast porcelain boxes with ceramic transfers of the 16th-century Agas map of London.
Contents of boxes from archaeologist Mike Webber and mudlarker Lara Maiklem

Bearebaytng
S Mary

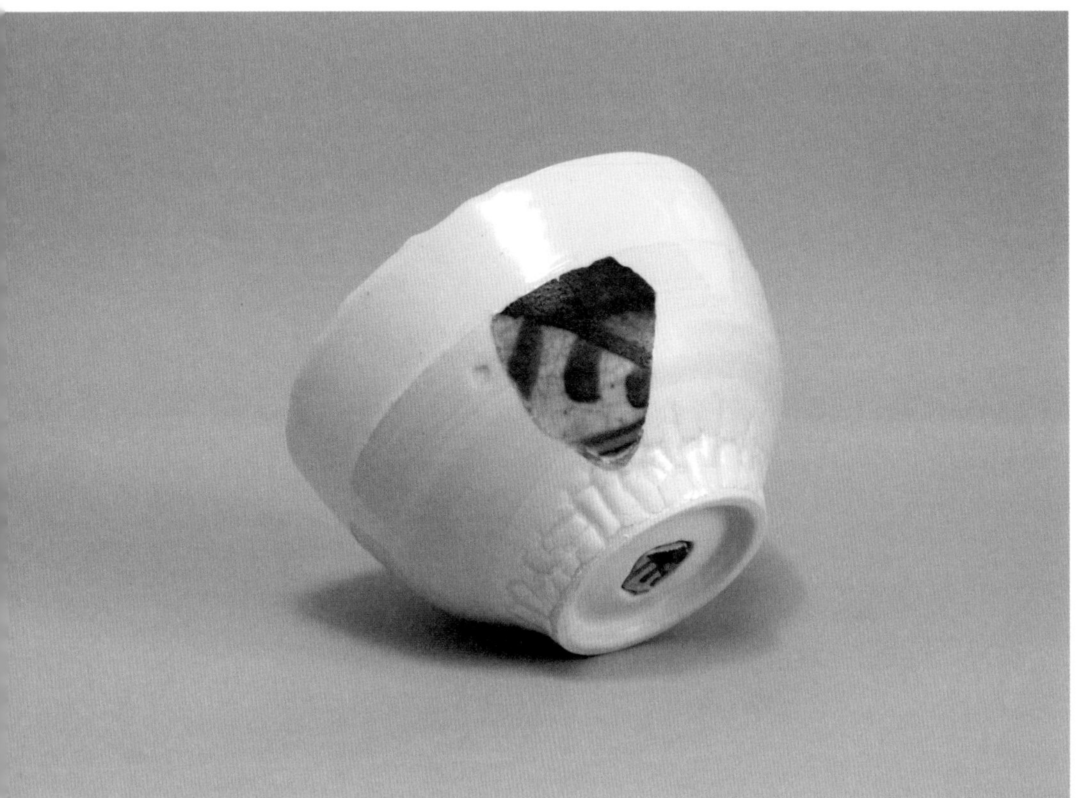

A Little Bit of Delft, 2019. Thrown porcelain with inserted Delft shard and ceramic transfer

Delft Mudlarking, 2020. Thrown porcelain with ceramic transfers

Mudlarking Bottle and Inkwell, 2020. Thrown porcelain with glass find inserted into the bottleneck and ceramic transfer fired on to a pipe stem

I like taking a discarded object and elevating its status by using porcelain.

Hans Tan

'In the Asian context, mending is not a profession that anyone aspires to,' says designer, maker and curator Hans Tan (1980, Singapore). 'I wanted to reposition repair as an explorational activity that could generate an inspirational outcome.' He set about doing so by curating an exhibition called *R for Repair* at Singapore's National Design Centre in early 2021, followed by a second exhibition at the Victoria & Albert Museum as part of the 2022 London Design Festival in collaboration with curator Jane Withers.

'As a child, coming from a middle-class family in Singapore, it was not uncommon to repair things when they broke. There was always an electrical repair shop nearby, and it was not unusual for clothes to be mended,' says Tan. 'On the other hand, coming from a Chinese family, my relationship with mending is complex. Buying something new is considered a sign of prosperity; for example, it was customary to receive a new set of clothes during Chinese New Year. In fact, there is a Chinese saying: If the old doesn't go, the new will not come.' Despite that complex relationship, as a designer-maker in Singapore where natural resources are scarce and craft fabricators are hard to find, using waste and found objects became a key part of Tan's own work. 'It's a matter of being clever with what is available,' he says. 'This way of working has evolved into an interest and a strategy in my practice, so a lot of what I do could be considered "repair" to some extent.'

The idea for *R for Repair* was born from a brief Tan wrote for industrial design students at the National University of Singapore.

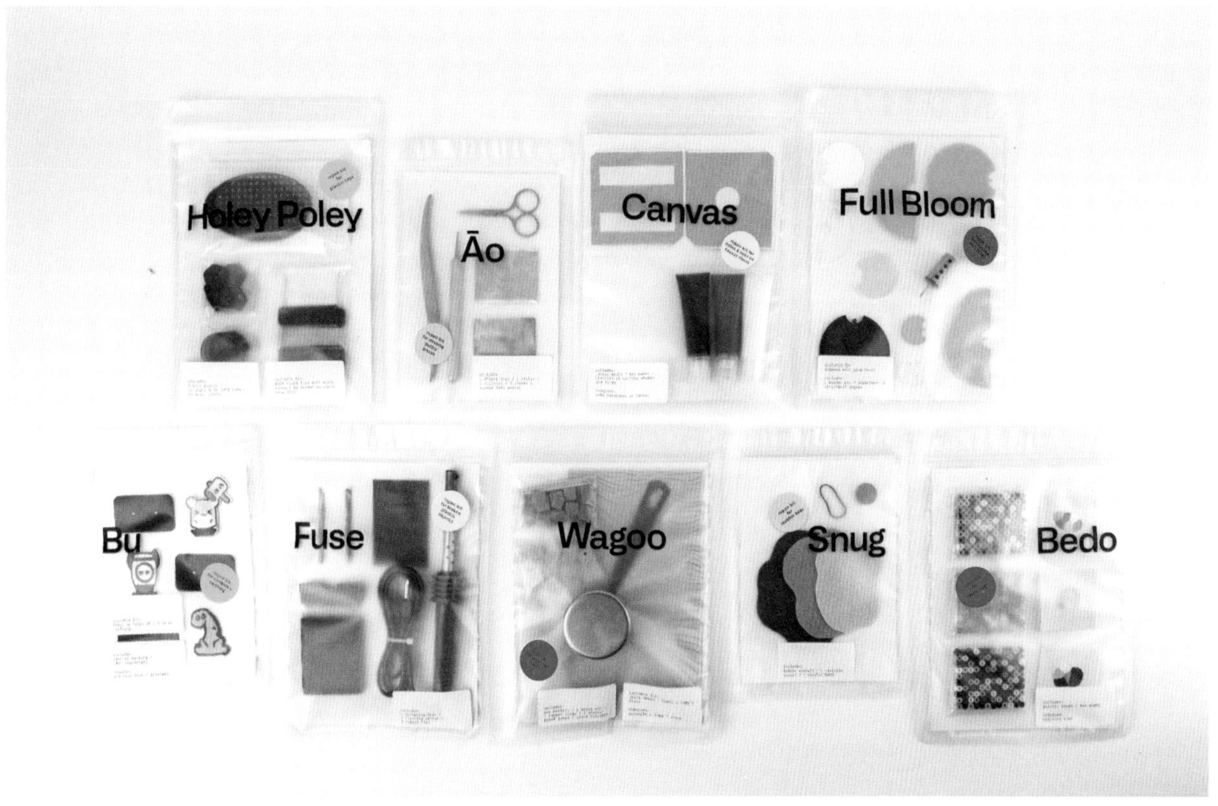

Repair kits designed by students from the department of industrial design, National University of Singapore

'I was reflecting on how people see repair as lesser compared to buying a new product,' he says. 'Repair is typically perceived as a demeaning profession and designers aspire to create new products. I thought it would be interesting to write a brief asking my students to "repair" that perspective.' Taking inspiration from the Japanese art of *kintsugi*, Tan asked his students to repair something so that it would end up better than its original state. They were also tasked with creating a kit and instructions to allow anyone to replicate their mend (above).

For the *R for Repair* exhibition, ten Singapore designers were paired with ten broken objects, each with personal significance to the member of the public who had volunteered it. A conversation with the object owner helped the designer learn about the value of the piece. 'I was hoping to get a variety of interpretations from the designers,' says Tan. 'I paired each designer with a product type they would feel comfortable experimenting with, but not too familiar.' He was clear in his brief that he was not looking for 'sustainable' solutions. 'Often, sustainable solutions are associated with inconvenience and sacrifice, so they don't result in a "sustainable" practice,' he says. 'To me, it was more important to look for a mindset shift, where their approaches provided different ways of seeing the concept of repair.' Tiffany Loy repaired a Calvin Klein tote bag that Arnold Goh had bought with his very first pay cheque. Once his pride and joy, it had developed holes and been relegated to use as a grocery bag. Loy repaired the holes with iron-on patches, turned the bag inside out (so that the holes were now on the inner fabric layer) and added a cord mesh to both strengthen the bag and act as an external pocket (p. 92). A personal object became a family object more suited to its new role.

Lin Ruiyin and Afzal Imram, founders of jewellery label State Property, were allocated an anklet gifted to its owner as a child. As she outgrew it, it broke and became unwearable. They took one of the original teddy bear links and used it to cast another – in gold with a diamond inserted on its heart – turning it into a bracelet for the wrist (pp. 90–91). 'That was a really thoughtful touch, because the repair brought attention to the broken part and elevated it,' says Tan. 'The repair really points to the heart of the piece, which is about its nostalgic value for the owner.'

A $15 Casio watch with a broken strap was the challenge presented to industrial design studio Lanzavecchia + Wai. It had already been through three battery replacements and a strap change, so its owner had finally replaced it with an identical one. Thus the watch's value was purely sentimental, but it still told the time. Framing the watch face in a cube made from solid walnut with a circular grain that matched the shape of the watch face, and brass pins carefully placed at the 3, 6, 9 and 12-hour points, turned it into a high-end bedside clock that could be cherished for years to come (p. 93).

'A totally different example is the ceramic cup with a broken handle, which was a family heirloom for a senior lady and her siblings,' says Tan. Instead of reattaching the handle, Atelier HOKO decided to sand down and protect the broken part, so that the mug would be safe and comfortable to use as it was (opposite). 'You can put the fullness of your hands over the cup when you are drinking tea, to feel the warmth, which could bring back memories associated with it,' explains Tan. 'It is beautiful because the repair invites the owner to be more considered about using it.' As for the handle, it was presented in a customised box to remind the owner that it is okay for things to be broken. 'Through storytelling, their concept positions the tea cup as "better than before" without an obvious repair intervention,' says Tan.

Each of these projects explores our relationship with the things we own, and it was those relationships the designers mended as much as the objects themselves. 'When you repair, you are working with something that has pre-existing conditions,' says Tan. 'These conditions could be a value, memory or reference, and while reshaping the object, you are inevitably reshaping those conditions. Therefore, it's a precious opportunity to use these conditions as elements that you can work with creatively, in tandem with materials and techniques.'

Tan set out to change the perception of repair, from something associated with poverty or the supposed sacrifices of sustainability, into something more positive. He wanted to position repair, not as an act of subsistence – something you do because you have to – but as an aspirational act of creativity. Did it work? '*R for Repair* has actually revealed an even broader perspective,' he says. 'And that is the significance of creativity and design to bring about change. The starting point of change is not behavioural, it begins with a shift in the way one perceives, and storytelling through repair is a really good way to do that.'

Repair is typically perceived as a demeaning profession and designers aspire to create new products. I thought it would be interesting to 'repair' that perspective.

Cup from Tan Geok Khim, repaired by Atelier HOKO

There is a Chinese saying: If the old doesn't go, the new will not come.

Bracelet from Yann Lee, repaired by State Property

Bag from Arnold Goh, repaired by Tiffany Loy

Watch from Nichole, repaired by Lanzavecchia + Wai

Repair as activism

Craftivism [noun] – the activity of using crafts (sewing or making things yourself using your hands) to try to achieve political or social change[1]

Injuries – to people, to communities, to the environment – no longer need to be repaired: they are not acknowledged, they are asked to disappear… in[to] the realm of the unthought, that which cannot be thought, formulated or expressed.

– Françoise Vergès[2]

'Craft' and 'activism' – words that sound like they belong on opposite ends of any spectrum: feminine to masculine, introversion to extroversion, compliance to rebellion, quiet and seated to shouting and marching. And yet here they are, squished together in the word 'craftivism' – a portmanteau coined by writer and maker Betsy Greer in 2003 to articulate the ways in which craft can be used as a form of protest. Her definition is broad: 'Craftivism is a way of looking at life where voicing opinions through creativity makes your voice stronger, your compassion deeper and your quest for justice more infinite.'[3] Artist and researcher Dr Tal Fitzpatrick has since honed the definition of craftivism as 'DIY citizenship' – a practice that empowers people to 'actively perform, test, rehearse and engage in the practice of democracy as part of their everyday lives' and in doing so 'materialise social, cultural and political change'.[4] The term 'DIY citizenship' comes from the title of a book by University of Toronto professor Matt Ratto;[5] he also calls it 'critical making' – a play on the words 'critical thinking' with the emphasis on hand instead of head.

The use of craft as a form of protest pre-dates this term. From banners and brooches to a silk handkerchief embroidered with the signatures of hunger strikers from prison, craft played an important part in the early 20th-century suffragette movement. Hand-stitched *arpilleras* (brightly coloured patchwork pictures) made by women in Chile during the 1973–90 military dictatorship were smuggled out of the country and used by Amnesty International to build public and political pressure to help bring down General Pinochet. And the NAMES Project AIDS Memorial Quilt comprises an ever-growing number of three by six feet (gravestone-sized) memorial panels, each made in honour of someone who died due to AIDS. The current quilt comprises 48,000 individual panels and is believed to be the largest piece of community folk art in the world.[6] 'The tension between these two levels – the quilt as a massive project versus the quilt as a product of intimate, local communities – is a major part of its complex effect,' writes Marita Sturken in her book *Tangled Memories*.[7] And it is this connection between intimate personal actions and large-scale social, cultural and political impact that gives craftivism its power.

Whereas craftivism has openly political aims, mending and repair activities are often nothing more than pragmatic in intent. But while motivations for mending may or may not be rooted in activism, the very act does take a stand of sorts. 'Repair has its own form and language of activism,' says artist and academic Bridget Harvey (p. 98). 'Repair-makers work both together and alone, stand against accepted consumption practices and educational hierarchies, and use their skills to work with damage, take stances, share and increase skills and independence.'[8]

The use of repair as an overt form of resistance is perhaps most obviously traced to the British Make Do & Mend initiative of the Second World War. Materials were diverted to the war effort, so mending clothes rather than buying new became a way for those left at home to show solidarity with soldiers on the front line – every darned stocking freeing up silk for parachutes. But while this was a mainstream government-led effort that (largely) united a country against a common enemy, it is within the 1980s punk movement that repair emerges as a counter-cultural form of protest.[9]

In an anti-fashion statement usually attributed to US punk musician Richard Hell,[10] punks appropriated safety pins from their domestic utilitarian context to 'repair' intentionally ripped clothes. 'The unemployed and semi-employed [had] been cast adrift, and for many young men and women, their attention... turned inwards towards the body,' explains cultural theorist Angela McRobbie. 'Wild peacock punk dressing of the type seen on the streets in the early 1980s signified this body politics, this making strange through an excessive marvellous, a "quotidian marvellous".'[11]

Subcultures such as punk use signs and symbols to signify their opposition to mainstream culture, to question what has been accepted as natural, and to reclaim their personal agency. 'By... subverting their conventional uses and inventing new ones, the subcultural stylist gives lie to... the false obviousness of everyday practice... and opens up the world of objects to new and covertly oppositional readings,' writes Dick Hebdige in *Subculture: The Meaning of Style*. 'The communication of a significant "difference" (and the parallel communication of group identity) then is the point behind the style of all spectacular subcultures.'[12] The punk movement was awash with signs and symbolism, some seemingly used for nothing more than to cause offence – but the intentionally torn clothes 'repaired' with safety pins challenged the idea that clothes in their perfect, undamaged state were 'natural' and that damage and repair were somehow 'unnatural'.

In the 40-odd years since the height of punk, the needle has once again superseded the safety pin, and the ways in which mending is used to challenge these accepted norms feel gentler than the shock tactics deployed by 1980s punks. To quote artist Louise Bourgeois, 'The needle is used to repair damage. It's a claim to forgiveness. It is never aggressive, it's not a pin.'[13] A new form of quiet activism is emerging. It is one that is inclusive of introverts and those who are 'historically reflexive and community-minded'[14] and is arguably just as effective at bringing about change. 'We need to stop seeing protest as only being about shouting in a crowd and start having the kind of smaller conversations that actually connect fellow human beings and help to influence them gently,' says Sarah Corbett, author of *How to be a Craftivist*.[15]

The repairers profiled in this chapter all demonstrate the power of what Bourgeois called 'the magic power of the needle,'[16] using mending techniques to challenge the status quo. Bridget Harvey's *Mend More* placard, made from a repaired jumper, formed part of a literal protest (p. 98). Paul Scott's ceramics (p. 104) represent 'critical making' on everything from fracking to modern slavery, while Paulo Goldstein (p. 122) offers outlandish but thought-provoking alternatives to the cult of consumerism. Aya Haidar's artworks (p. 112) document refugees' journeys and mothers' invisible labour and Claudia Clare's broken and reassembled pots (p. 130) tell stories of sexual violence against women. All these repairs are a form of activism – they subvert the spectrums by shouting quietly, embracing both movement and stillness, and enabling introverts to reclaim their personal agency and signify their opposition to the many ills of modern culture. Perhaps most importantly, they all acknowledge injuries to people, to communities and to the environment. If we let them, they will help to make our voices stronger, our compassion deeper and our quest for justice more infinite.

Bridget Harvey

Bridget Harvey

When you think about activism, the image that often springs to mind is one of protesters marching down a street holding placards. That's rarely the role that mending plays, but Bridget Harvey (1980, Colchester, UK) brought together her professional status as an artist, a mender and a 're-maker' with her identity as a 'staunch environmentalist and activist' in her *MEND MORE Jumper* (p. 103). 'It is part encouragement and part disparagement,' she says. 'Its stance is political: overt, visible, legible, unmistakable.' The purple acrylic jumper is embellished with hand-stitched yellow letters made from fabric scraps to spell out 'Mend More Bin Less' on one side and 'Mend More Buy Less' on the other. She carried the jumper on a pole with a top shaped like a coat hanger during the Global Climate March in London in 2015 (p. 102). '*MEND MORE Jumper* asks people to use repair skills for practicality, resilience and resistance, and to protect the planet,' she says. 'But is also carries a second-order message. It was something else before and now is new; it is critical, political, subversive and affirmative, its power intensified by its previous life. More than its graphics, its material supports its message.' Harvey is keen to point out that mending more and binning less has to be led by choice, not by oppression. 'Clothing repair has a strong relationship with women's history and domestic labour,' she says. 'As part of the reskilling movement, we are *choosing* to relearn these skills and encouraging others to relearn them and use them too. In order to become part of what American author and journalist Emily Matchar calls "the new domesticity" – reacting against the reduction of domesticity into convenience, and "longing for a more authentic, meaningful life in an environmentally and economically uncertain world".'

This thoughtful nuance is typical of Harvey's work, of which her *MEND MORE Jumper* is the most obvious, but far from the only example of mending as activism, and also of many other things besides. She often explains her practice by saying that she uses making to ask critical questions, generating new understanding and adding meaning through craft. 'I ask what we make, how we make it, and why that matters,' she says. Perhaps a less overt, but no less political piece is her *Blue Jumper*, found in pristine condition second-hand and repeatedly worn and darned as it became more and more moth-eaten over time. 'My stitched intervention acts as a placard: my slogan not shouted but darned,' she says. 'I can, I will, I am – through choice and necessity – wearing, repairing and re-wearing.' The fact that both sweaters have been acquired by London's Victoria & Albert Museum validates the cultural relevance of both types of activism – the marched and shouted as well as the quietly darned.

Harvey's practice is interdisciplinary and as well as working in used knitwear, she also repairs and remakes damaged ceramics. 'I have always worked with reclaimed materials, but specifically I have found that these common objects are both interesting to work with and useful media through which to translate my ideas,' she says. 'It was while working on my *Blue Jumper* that I realised that mending went beyond being a chore to being a practical stance for environmentalism, a political stance against consumerism, and a creative act with a variety of aesthetic choices. Ceramics are an interesting medium that isn't commonly mended – I had been reading about repair methods that had fallen out of use, and many of them were on domestic ceramics, so I decided to start experimenting with them.'

One of the techniques Harvey read about dates from the 19th century and involves boiling broken ceramics in cow's milk to repair cracks and breakages. Despite being vegan and not believing for a moment it would work, she decided to give it a try. 'I wanted to "re-story" this forgotten practice, to bring it back as a focus,' she explains, although her husband – also vegan – did request that she open all the kitchen windows before she got started. She selected a shattered cereal bowl 'which may have contained its fair share of milk before its demise', bound the fragments together with wire and submerged the whole thing in four pints of milk in an old wok, then boiled the milk for four hours. She left it to cool completely, then removed the bowl from the milk. 'The bowl looked exactly the same –

Harvey repairing ceramics in her studio, 2021 (above and opposite)

the wire was intact, compelling its shards into shape,' she says. 'I could see a shiny gloop in some of the craters, but aside from that, there was no visual change. Snipping the wire, I realised that the bowl was whole again, with little evidence of its former smashed self. Peculiarly, it did not smell – despite the aroma in our kitchen – and the only evidence of its milky adventure was a plasticky residue on some of its surface.'

She also mixes materials more visually: 'I draw my techniques and ideas from a variety of sources because, by its very nature, repair is an interdisciplinary subject,' she says. For *Red Blanket, Blue Bowl, Wrench* she patched a blanket with flattened tin cans, connected two halves of a broken bowl with beadwork and left the wrench untouched. 'Objects gifted to me by women: two are repaired semi-functionally and one awaits its fix,' she says. 'Visibly damaged and visibly repaired, they represent care and effort, destruction and addition of narrative via remaking and repair, conservation of objects of cultural insignificance.' Technically, two of these domestic objects are mended, none of them fulfil their original function and yet, somehow, all three have been elevated from ordinary to extraordinary. 'Through practical and impractical repair techniques, I create provocative objects to help us talk about repair and think about how we can enact it on a wider basis,' says Harvey. 'By also talking and writing about my work, exhibiting it and running workshops, I help to share the ideas that inspire it.'

Whether it's protesting on the streets, quietly darning moth holes in her own clothes, or creating pieces that surprise us and disrupt our expectations of what is possible or sensible, Harvey is challenging the status quo and asking us all to do something different in the face of climate crisis – something hopeful. 'Repair is a point where hope as disposition meets hope in material practice,' she says. 'We would not attempt a repair if we were not hoping for resolution to a problem.'

I ask what we make, how we make it, and why that matters.

MEND MORE Jumper carried on the Global Climate March in London, 2015

MEND MORE Jumper, 2015

MEND MORE Jumper asks people to use repair skills for practicality, resilience and resistance, and to protect the planet.

Paul Scott

As an artist, author and educator, Paul Scott (1953, Darley Dale, UK) subverts the comforting familiarity of traditional blue-and-white transferware with images depicting social, environmental and political concerns. These range from the Seascale pigeons – radioactive birds that once came and went from Sellafield nuclear power station – to the civil war and unfolding humanitarian crisis in Syria – all within the recognisable aesthetic of the pastoral scenes and floral motifs associated with the discipline.

He used to rely on overprinting factory seconds, but found that his supply dried up when ceramics production moved overseas and many of the factories in the UK's pottery heartland of Stoke-on-Trent closed. He started buying 19th-century plates and platters, but could only afford broken and damaged ones. 'I grew up in Birmingham, so I've always been interested in industrial decay and urban decline – and it's a theme that runs through the 19th-century obsession with ruins,' he says. 'I had this beautiful platter from about 1830 with a crack running from the bottom right up to the middle of the plate. At the time, I was working on a series to do with fracking, and I suddenly thought, "Well, that's actually quite good, isn't it?"' He sought the advice of curators, ceramics restorers and art historians about how to stabilise the plate. After one responded with: 'No, no, no, you can't. You can't do things like that. Those old ways of repairing interfere with the integrity of the object. Even if I knew how to do it, I would never tell you,' he decided to teach himself. He found a copy of *China Mending & Restoration* by Parsons and Curl, published by Faber &

Paul Scott

Faber in 1963, and learned the basics of *kintsugi.* With a little help from the metalwork department at the Oslo National Academy of the Arts, where he was a visiting professor, he also learned to use staples and rivets to connect broken parts – itself a technique with a rich if controversial history in ceramics conservation.

Cumbrian Blue(s), New American Scenery, Fracked No: 02/21 (p. 107) depicts a hydraulic frack pump on the horizon – all in blue – with the gold *kintsugi* crack running up from the bottom of the platter to the pump, representing the damage it is doing to the earth beneath. 'Fracking damages the earth – the crack releases gas and oil, which makes some people very rich, but it really damages the planet,' he says. 'I am very much against your nuclear power, fracking, coal-fired power stations, the rest of it... we are fucking the planet, big time. The older I get, the more I despair at what we're doing, so my interventions in my ceramics are trying to bring people's attention to that.'

From the starting point of affordability to this neat coincidence, mending, repair and reuse have become integral to Scott's practice. 'Reusing historical material gives the artworks extra resonance,' he says. 'Because the object already has a story, then another layer was added when it was damaged or broken, I'm just adding another layer on top of that. So, the process is conceptually significant, but in the wider sense, mending is something humans have done for thousands of years. It's only very recently that we've stopped repairing things, and it's completely unsustainable.'

Today, Scott continues to buy 19th-century plates and platters to use as his 'canvases'. He starts by firing them to find out what will happen to them at such high temperatures – if a piece if going to crack, he wants to know about it upfront. He then creates his designs using his own photography or images from newsreels (with permission from the original photographers) and collages them together – using an old machine that runs a now-discontinued Photoshop filter that gives his artwork files the appearance of engravings – before screen-printing decals to lay on to the plates before firing them again. Having printed the decals by hand for decades, he is beginning to experiment with digital printing. Then, finally, he makes any repairs to the pieces using glue and gold leaf.

As well as using mending and repair to reflect on environmental issues, Scott also makes work about issues of social injustice, such as a tea service in memory of the Chinese cockle pickers who drowned in Morecambe Bay in 2004, made to commemorate the anniversary of the abolition of slavery – as an ironic commentary on the continuation of the practice in the modern age. His *Syria Series* subverts the traditional blue-and-white ware aesthetic with scenes from the civil war and ongoing humanitarian crisis there, while his *Cumbrian Blue(s), Bombs Over Baghdad* (pp. 108–109) remains shattered, its broken state telling us more than a repair ever could. 'Environmentalism and social justice are inextricably tied together,' he explains. 'The Western capitalist system creates inequality in the process of killing the planet – it's completely unsustainable. I am working on a series about the Hudson River at the moment and industrialisation has poisoned that river to the extent that it's not going back to its natural state for many, many, many years, if ever. It's all connected – there's an arrogance in the Western philosophy that needs to change.'

Is he hopeful about the future? Does he believe that change will come? 'No, not

Scott applying screen-printed ceramic transfers to an antique pearlware platter

Front and back views of *Cumbrian Blue(s), New American Scenery, Fracked No: 02/21 (01/12/11/21)*. Transfer print collage on broken earthenware platter c. 1920, with *kintsugi* repair, 2021

really,' he laughs. 'Some days, I get terribly depressed, but then, people in power rely on that fatalism, and on other days, you do see things changing. So, I oscillate between thinking things are completely fucked and finding a little bit of hope. I think the key is to focus on what you can control. I might feel completely helpless in the light of worldwide events, but what I can do is impact my immediate environment – through my art, I can have a small impact on what people see in museums and galleries, and hopefully open their eyes a little. When people see my work, they see it on one level, and then suddenly spot the nuclear power station in the landscape. There's a dawning realisation that all is not as it seems. That double-take enables them to see a whole genre of objects – and even situations – in a new light. It's sort of enlightening.'

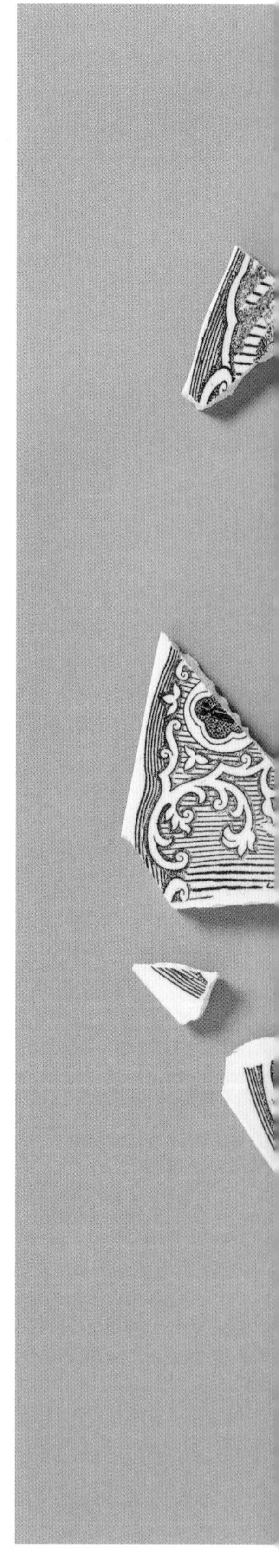

Cumbrian Blue(s), Bombs Over Baghdad. Transfer print collage on broken handmade ceramic platter, 2003–12

I might feel completely helpless in the light of worldwide events, but what I can do is impact my immediate environment.

Front (above) and back (opposite) views of *Cumbrian Blue(s), Fukushima No: 3*. Transfer print collage on broken and reassembled Willow pattern platter, marked 'Japan' (c. 1965). Wave insert from erased Willow platter (c. 1840), with *kintsugi* repair, 2014

Mending is something humans have done for thousands of years. It's only very recently that we've stopped repairing things, and it's completely unsustainable.

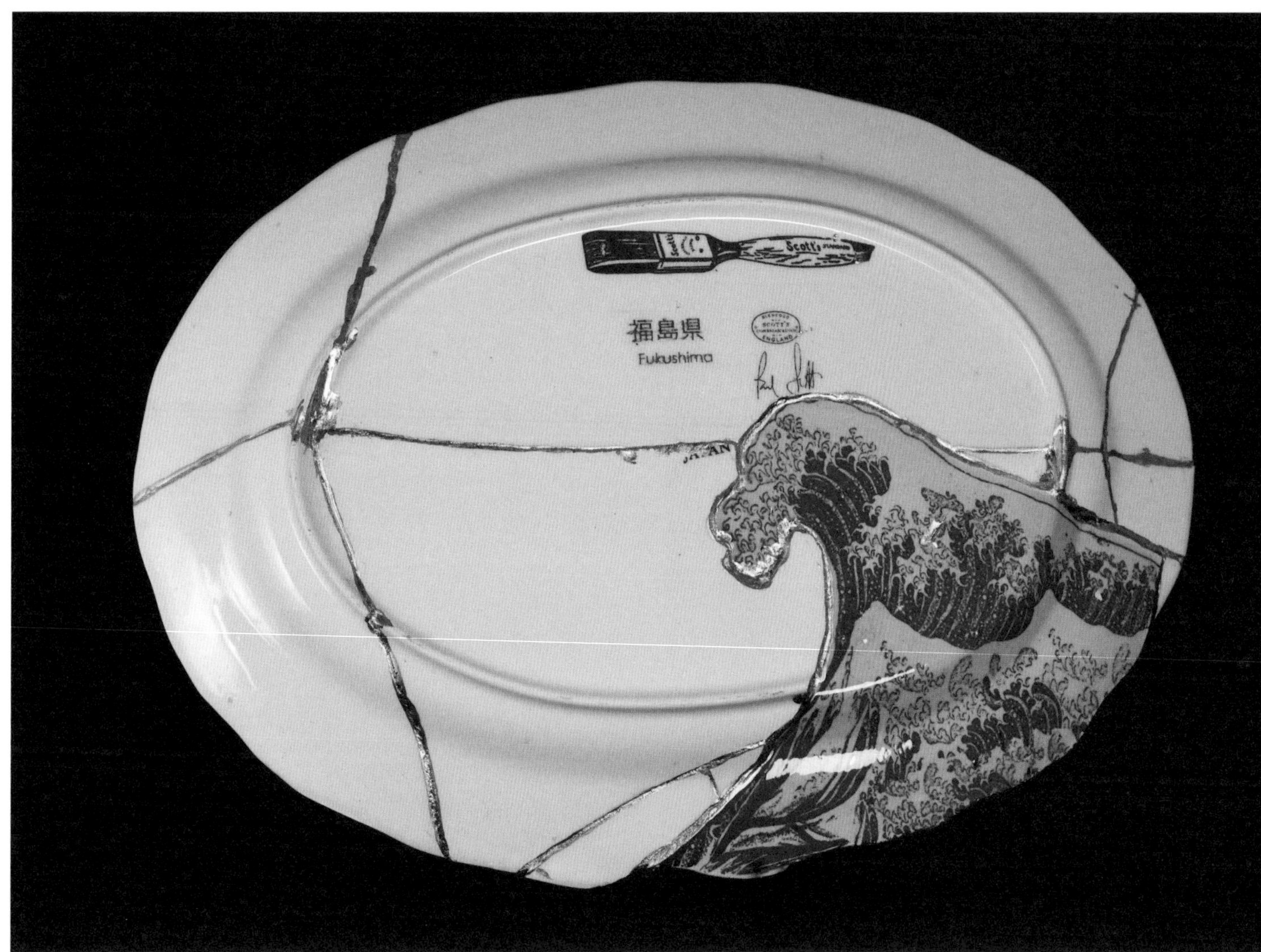

Aya Haidar

Aya Haidar

'Repair wasn't some special craft activity we did on the side,' says Lebanese-British artist Aya Haidar (1985, Houston, Texas, US). 'As I was having my after-school snack, my grandma would be mending; as I was doing my homework, she would be threading needles; as I was getting ready for bed, she would be patching clothes – and all the while telling me stories about Lebanon, about the war, about politics and society, about our family heritage.' Haidar was born in the US into a Lebanese family. She lived in Saudi Arabia until she was six and was then raised in London with a Muslim upbringing and a French education. Through it all, she remembers her grandmother mending. And that is something she has inherited – in fact, she is raising four children without buying anything new. From clothes and toys to school bags and bikes, everything they own has been sourced second-hand, handed down or shared among friends, neighbours and members of online 'swap groups' in Hackney, London. 'I think the stronger the community you live in, the less you need to live a disposable lifestyle,' she says. And keeping objects in use for longer means more repairs, which, for Haidar, only adds to their value. 'It's about the time and love my grandmother and my mom put into mending things for me and that I now put into mending things for my children.'

In a throw-away society, any form of repair could be seen as a form of activism, but as an artist, Haidar's labours of love take on extra resonance. In the same way that her grandmother's mending came laden with stories, her own work explores themes of diaspora, displacement and forced migration and is infused with intergenerational, interpersonal stories. For *Highly Strung* (pp. 115–117), she noted down one of the many acts of invisible labour she undertook each day, for a whole year – from physical acts such as vacuuming, to mental undertakings such as remembering 'to pack the *blue* towel for swimming,' to bodily exploits such as producing breast milk for her newborn baby. She hand-embroidered each of these 365 acts on to relevant objects, such as stained muslins, dirty dish rags, old school uniforms – all things that had outlived their useful life within her own home. Without restoring their former function, she gave each object new life, filling a gallery space by hanging them on washing lines, strung at eye level. 'Walking through the installation was an immersive experience that could feel overwhelming and claustrophobic for adults, many of whom came out feeling suffocated by this never-ending walkway of chores,' she says. 'And yet, it was at such a height that children could run and play beneath it with all of this literally going over their heads – there was something quite beautiful about that visual metaphor.' She priced the work to reflect minimum wage multiplied by 24 hours and then by 365 days.

Another work, *Hard Labour* (p. 118) and *Soft Labour* (p. 119), saw her embellish the stains on a cleaning rag (hard labour) and a muslin cloth that had been used for burping a baby (soft labour) using hand embroidery. Both *Highly Strung* and these pieces came out of an artist residency during which she worked with migrant domestic workers and also gave birth to her third child, prompting an exploration of the vulnerability as well as the invisible labour of motherhood. 'I wanted to highlight the marks on these cloths, so I stitched these colourful, vibrant patterns that look like explosive flowers around them,' she says. 'There is this requirement in our society to keep your house clean and tidy – everything has to be pristine and look brand-new – but that is really just hiding the records of our labour, the records of life. When the baby pukes on a burp cloth, it leaves a yellowy stain even once the cloth is clean, but this is a record of me having produced breast milk, it is a record of my baby being satiated and fed by me – it's visceral and raw, but it's also very honest.' The 'veneration of newness'[1] that consumer culture promotes not only erases domestic labour, but it is also completely unsustainable from an environmental perspective. 'I look back at how my grandmother used to mend and darn and sew and stitch and there's so much more value in that, because there is consideration of how you can make things fit together to give them a new lease of life.'

For *Soleless* (pp. 120–121), Haidar worked with anthropologist Mark Higgins on a European Social Fund-supported project to help 120 Syrian refugee families integrate into life in a rural town near Aberdeen, Scotland. As the only Arabic speaker and a mother of two young children who was far from home herself, Haidar became someone the women refugees could confide in. She shares their stories not to evoke pity but because she believes they need to be heard, from the women whose crying baby was thrown overboard from an overcrowded dingy crossing the Mediterranean to keep the other passengers from being caught, to the man who carried his three children – one on his back, one on his shoulders and one in a sling – on the long, gruelling walk from Greece to Germany. As well as bearing witness to these stories, Haidar embroiders them into the soles of the worn-out shoes in which the refugees crossed borders to reach safety. 'The wear and tear and the dirt and marks are as much a part of the journeys they've endured as the visual representation of their stories that I have added. They create a much more profound body of work that can really touch someone,' she says. 'These interpersonal revelations can help to humanise this group of people, as we realise that they are parents just like so many of us.' Forced migration is only going to increase with climate change; Haidar's work is an important reminder of the humanity of those already displaced.

As a self-described 'mother, artist and humanitarian,' Haidar has woven reuse and repair into every aspect of her life and work. 'There's something so powerful about mending and repair in environmental activism and other types of intersecting activism such as equality and social justice,' she says. 'The personal agency that comes with repair goes against consumerism and represents a challenge to a broken system. If there's going to be any sustainable long-term change, everyone needs to take into account this responsibility and negotiate a bit of personal agency for themselves.'

1 Susan Strasser, *Waste and Want: A Social History of Trash* (New York: Henry Holt & Co., 1999), 5.

Highly Strung, 2021, Guggenheim Collection (here exhibited at Cromwell Place, South Kensington, London, 2–9 June 2021)

Everything has to be pristine and look brand-new – but that is really just hiding the records of our labour, the records of life.

The personal agency that comes with repair goes against consumerism and represents a challenge to a broken system.

Highly Strung, 2021, Guggenheim Collection (here exhibited at Cromwell Place, South Kensington, London, 2–9 June 2021)

Highly Strung, 2021, Guggenheim Collection (here exhibited at Cromwell Place, South Kensington, London, 2–9 June 2021)

Hard Labour, 2019

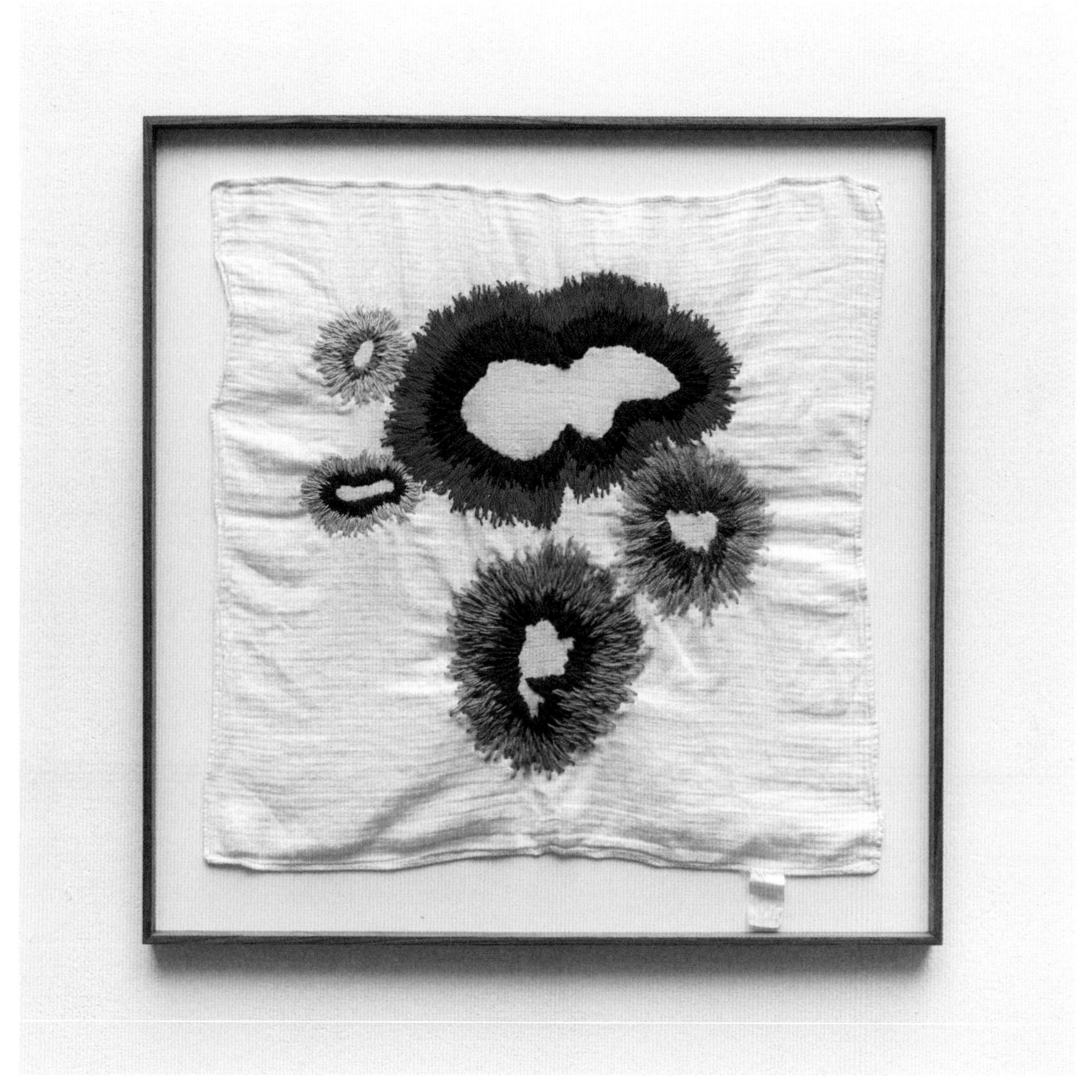

Soft Labour, 2019

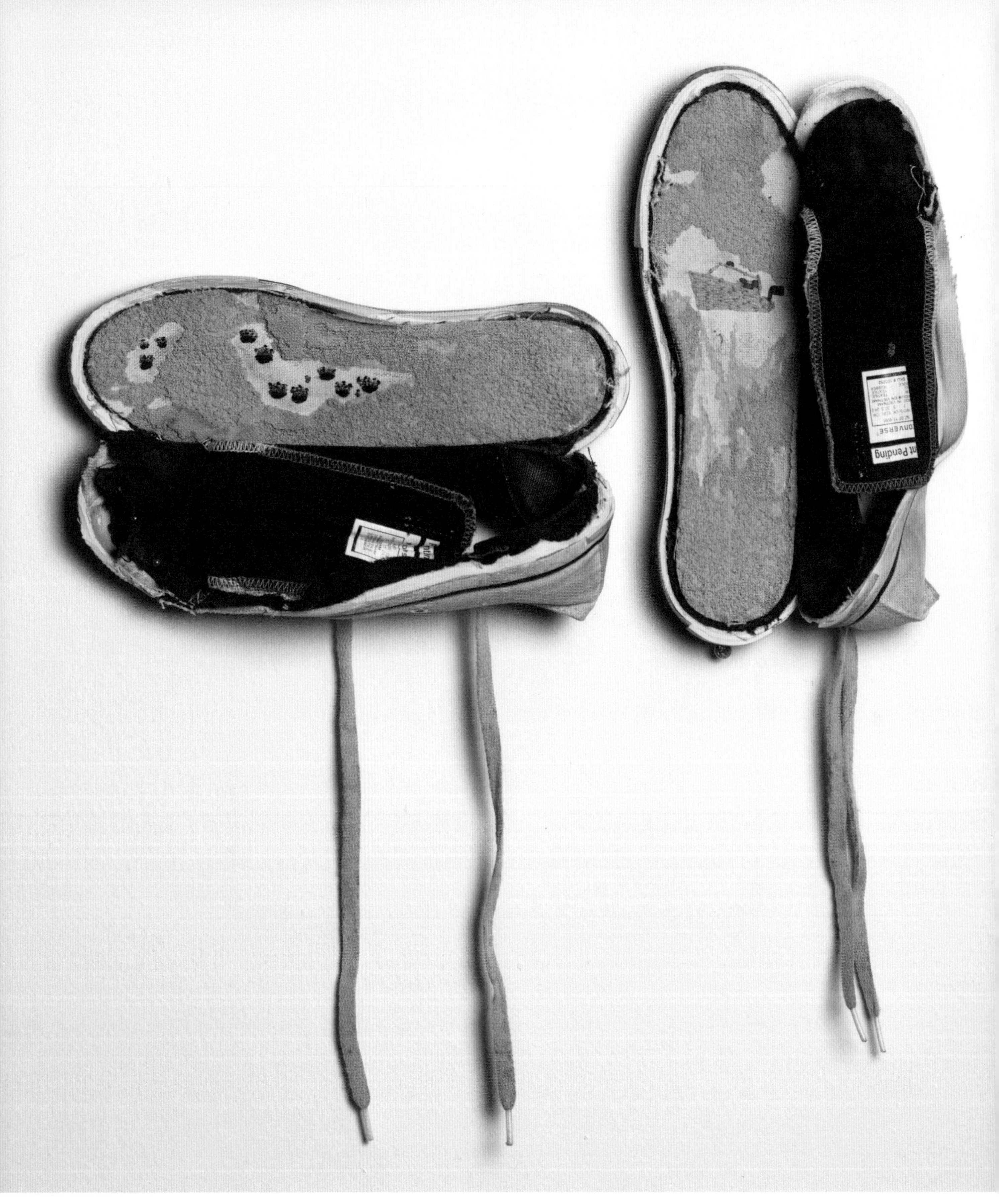

Patrol, 2018, from the series *Soleless*

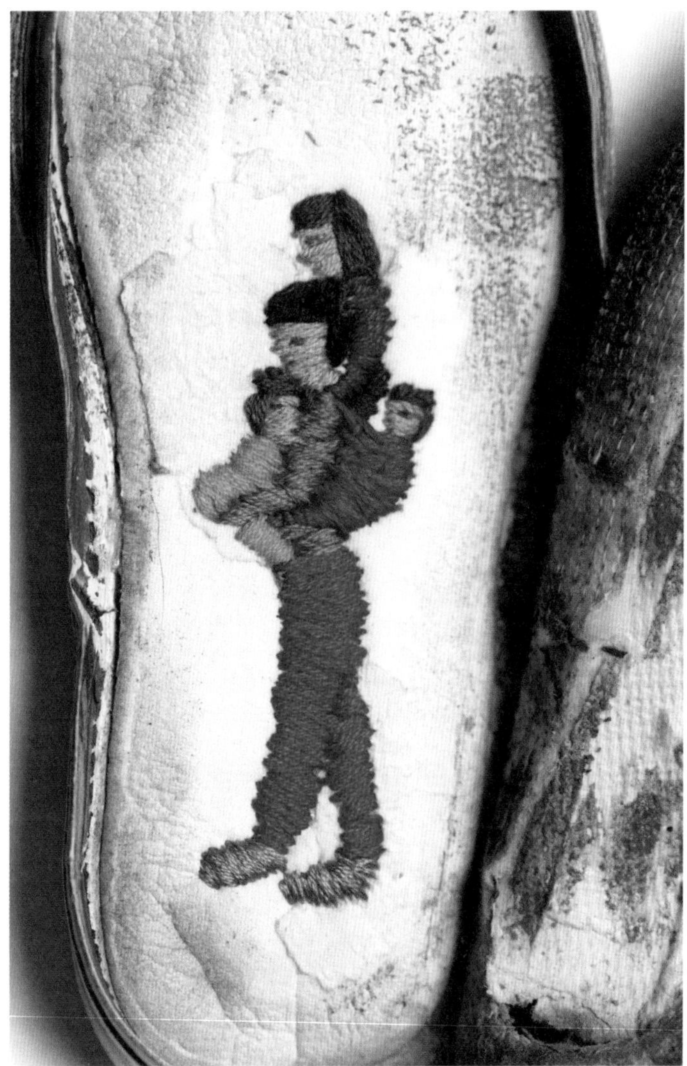

He Walked, 2018, from the series *Soleless*

Paulo Goldstein

Describing himself as a craftsman and a designer trying to stay true to his values while 'paddling against the current', Paulo Goldstein (1980, São Paulo, Brazil) reveals that repair is close to his heart. Having grown up in a family where everything was either mended, repurposed or passed on, he cites his grandfather who 'repaired everything with epoxy putty', his grandmother who mended clothes, and time spent in his father's home workshop as inspirations. 'The combination of these realities and opportunities made a lot possible, initially in terms of repair and then in creating,' he says. But whereas his family's repair was largely driven by thrift, his work has taken on a more political patina.

'A broken object delivers frustration because it doesn't achieve its functionality, but the same principle applies to the broken system that caused the financial crisis, which has affected our lives since 2008,' he said in 2013, arguing that taking repairs into our own hands in times of uncertainty can give us a feeling of control 'by scaling a major societal problem down to a human size, and projecting frustration upon broken objects that can be repaired through design and craftsmanship'.

Goldstein graduated in fine art from São Paulo's Fundação Armando Alvares Penteado (FAAP) in 2003, then worked as an illustrator for children's books and magazines before moving into stop motion as a sculptor and pattern maker on projects for filmmakers Wes Anderson and Tim Burton. In 2012, he completed a master's degree in industrial design at Central Saint Martins in London. His graduate project, entitled Repair is Beautiful, tackled the relationship between broken objects and broken systems.

Deploying self-taught or adapted skills and whatever materials he could lay his hands on, he mounted the constituent elements of an iPod shuffle on to a spare-rib bone salvaged from a university meal (p. 124), fixed a broken headphone with a shoulder-mount (p. 127, left), and an Anglepoise lamp with an exaggerated wooden wheel at the hinge (p. 126). He also used techniques borrowed from suspension bridges and mast rigging to restore the functionality of a director's chair. The aesthetic is two-parts *gambiarra*, one-part steampunk and one-part Heath Robinson. By challenging conventions, he invites us to question norms too. 'The final outcome was a collection of intriguingly repaired objects imbued with new meaning and functionality,' he says. 'The once-rejected objects reflect the environment that created them and call us to question our society as a whole.'

Professor Jeremy Till, then head of Central Saint Martins, commissioned Goldstein to bring life to an unoccupied space in the university's new building at Kings Cross, posing the question 'What if instead of adding, one redistributes what is there already?' The pair scoured the streets of London for discarded objects and Goldstein repurposed them to create the Scarcity project – a 'front parlour' welcoming visitors to the building (pp. 128–129). Using scarcity

Paulo Goldstein sitting on his *Magrela Chair* at MADE design fair in São Paulo, 2017

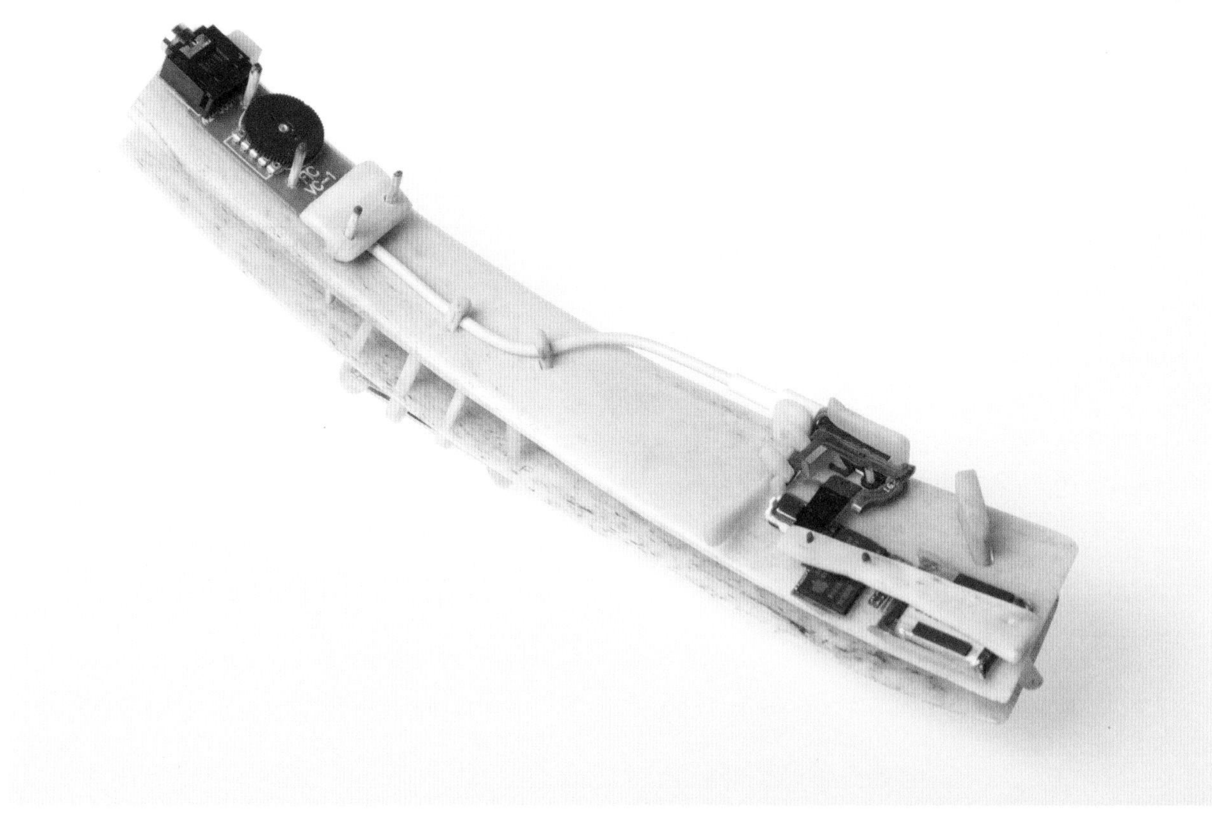

Repaired IPod Shuffle, part of the Repair is Beautiful project, London, 2012

as a springboard for creativity, chairs, sofas, tables and sideboards were repaired with pieces of other chairs, sofas, tables and sideboards – plus 300 metres of rope. 'Austerity is a political condition justified by scarcity,' says Goldstein. 'And it is normally seen as lack or limitation of resources, but is scarcity really a limitation or is it more a matter of perception and context?' When we think about what we need to do to bring about a more sustainable future, we also tend to think about sacrifice and lack. We can get trapped in a zero-sum game – the notion that if one person wins, someone else has to lose. By finding value in the wealth of discarded material goods that consumerism leaves in its wake, Goldstein demonstrated the opposite – abundance – and a new perspective. In their book *The Future We Choose*, Christiana Figueres and Tom Rivett-Carnac argue that 'endless abundance' is one of three mindsets we need to adopt in the face of the climate crisis: 'Faced with the ultimate scarcity, we must internalise the new zero-sum (either we all win or we all lose) and apply a mindset of abundance to that which we have left and that which we can co-create and share.'[1] Although Goldstein's project predates the book, it epitomises exactly this kind of thinking.

In 2018, Goldstein created a solo exhibition for São Paulo's Galeria Nicoli. 'I see my work as a collection of different chapters or layers talking about design, craftmanship, form and function,' he says. 'Sometimes that's from a critical point of view; sometimes exploring and experimenting; and sometimes it's just exercising technique, honing skill.' This project feels like the latter, but is no

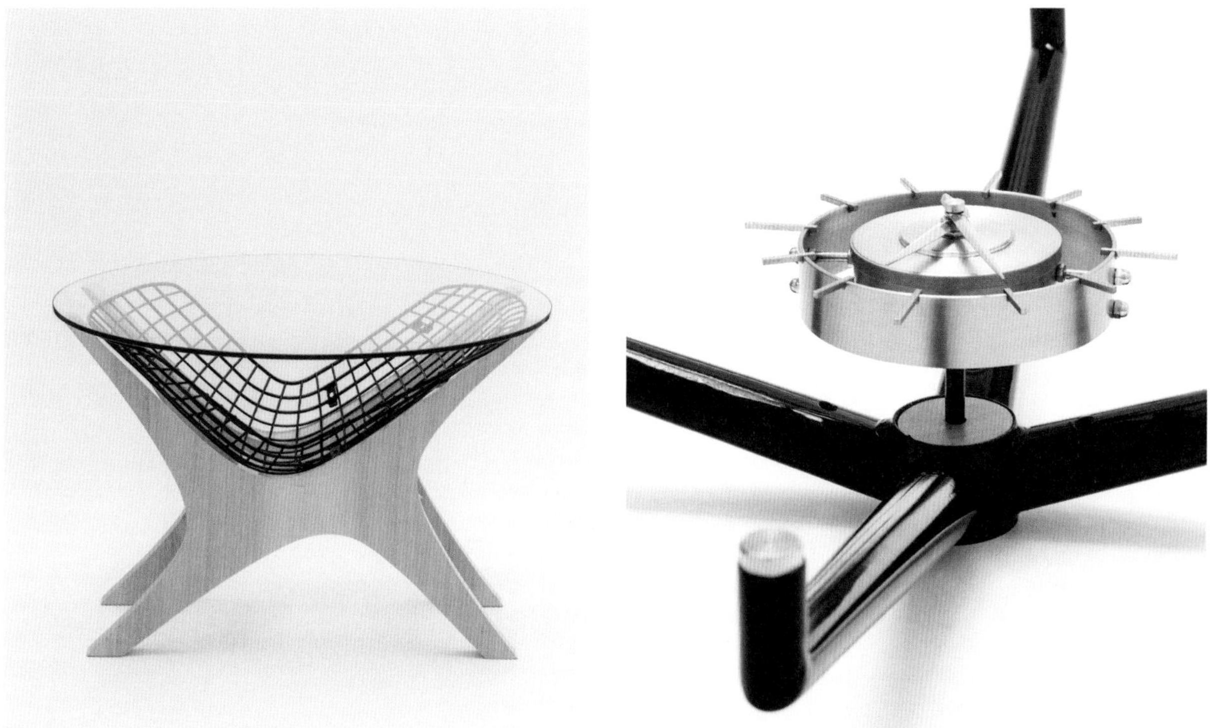

Collateral Coffee Table and *Collateral Clock*, part of the solo exhibition *Collateral Design* at Galeria Nicoli, São Paulo, 2018

less powerful for it. He took seven found objects (rendered in black) and created new functionality for them by adding bespoke elements – such as wooden legs and a glass top to an iconic designer chair-back that transformed them into a table, or a clockface to an office chair base that turned it into a decorative wall clock (above). 'I tend to organise the discarded objects I find side by side as a collection, grouping them in my studio by material or colour or function, and then, after looking at them for hours – or days – an idea might come to me,' he says. 'In this project, I wanted to explore that unintentional design; the collateral result of the forms that attract me.'

Whether he is taking a critical viewpoint, or simply exploring ideas, the theme that runs through Goldstein's work is always about staying true to his values while challenging the status quo. 'It is a matter of changing the throwaway mindset, the low-quality products, the fast-everything consumption,' he says. 'I believe quality and durability should be more easily accessible, or at least we should be able to access and open our objects so we can fix or replace broken parts – but first, the most difficult step is to fix the broken society mindset of produce, consume and discard.' When I first interviewed Goldstein almost a decade ago, I asked him what he was most proud of. 'That I tried,' was his somewhat modest answer. If we are to bring about genuine change, more of us need to join him in 'paddling against the current', so that he's not the only one.

1 Christina Figueres & Tom Rivett-Carnac, *The Future We Choose: Surviving The Climate Crisis* (London: Manilla Press, 2020), 78.

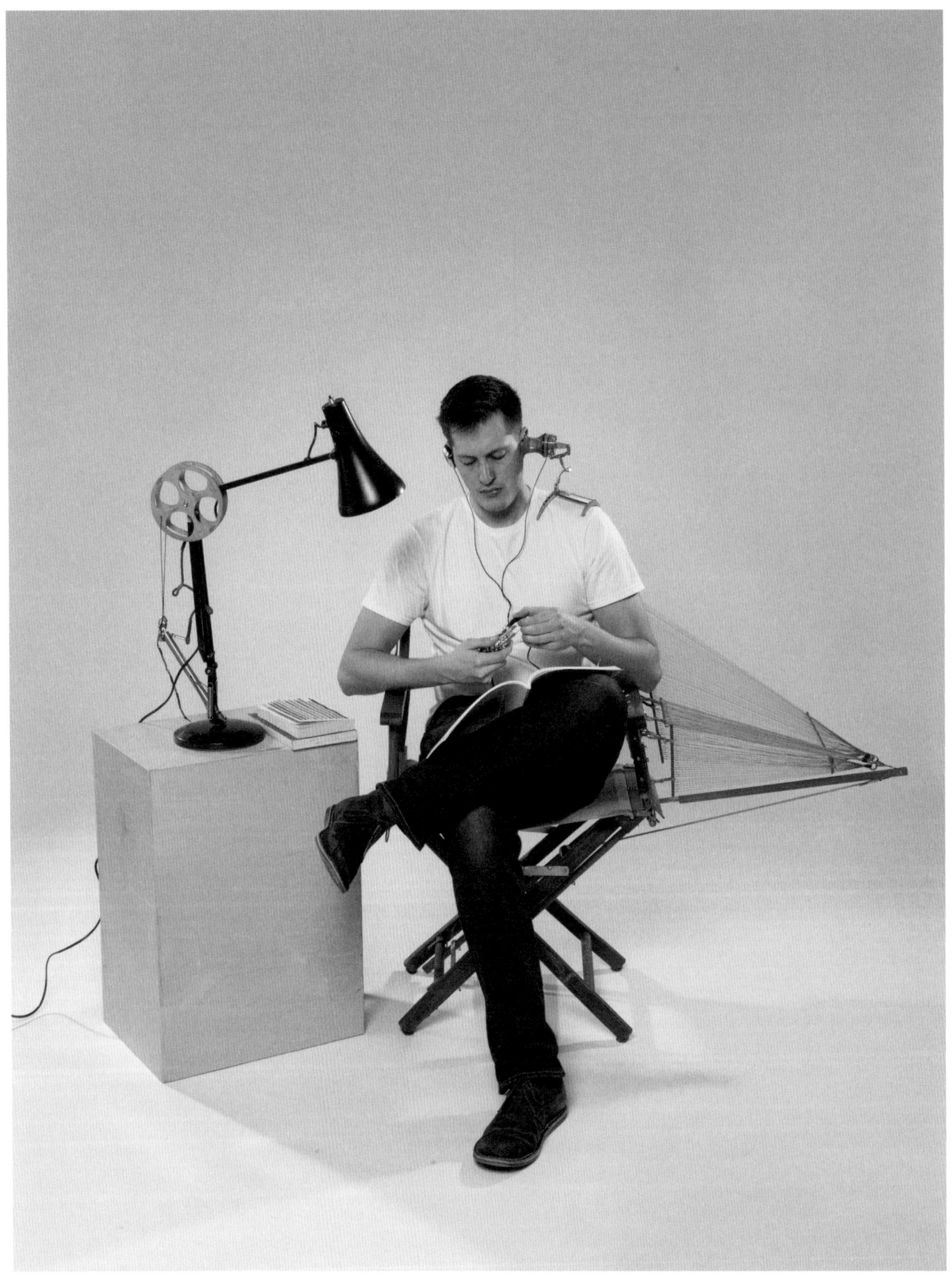

Paulo Goldstein's Repair is Beautiful project, London, 2012

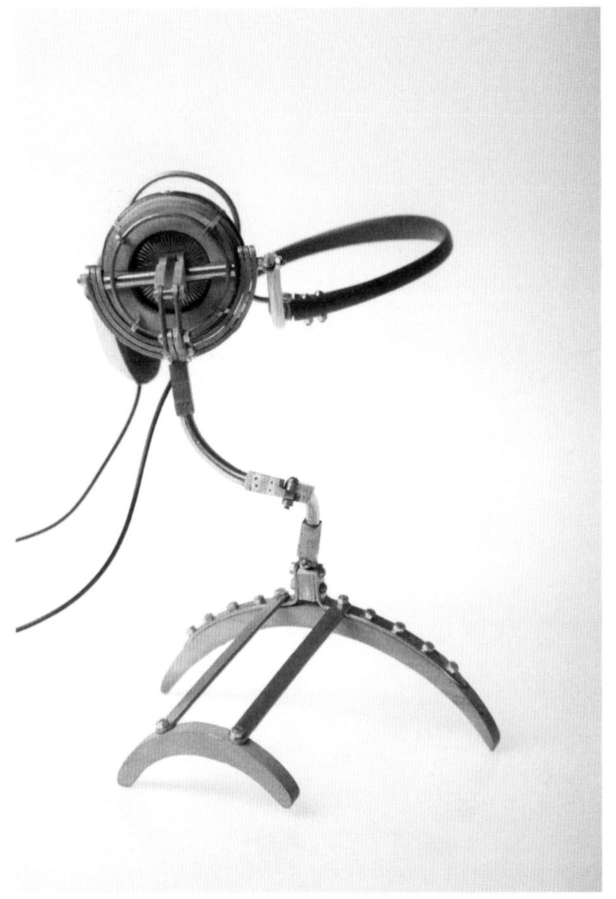

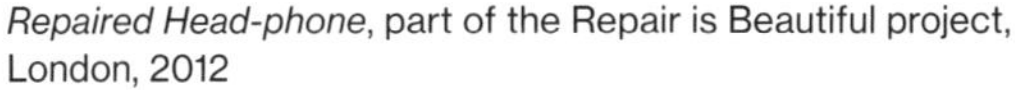

Repaired Head-phone, part of the Repair is Beautiful project, London, 2012

Repaired Garden Chair, continuation of the Repair is Beautiful project, London/São Paulo, 2013

Quality and durability should be easier to access, but first the most difficult step is to fix the broken society mindset of produce, consume and discard.

Several chairs of the Scarcity project, London, 2013: *Camden Chair*, *Islington Chair*, *Hackney Chair*, *Angel Chair*. Each chair was assembled from random pieces of discarded furniture and materials, collected from around London.

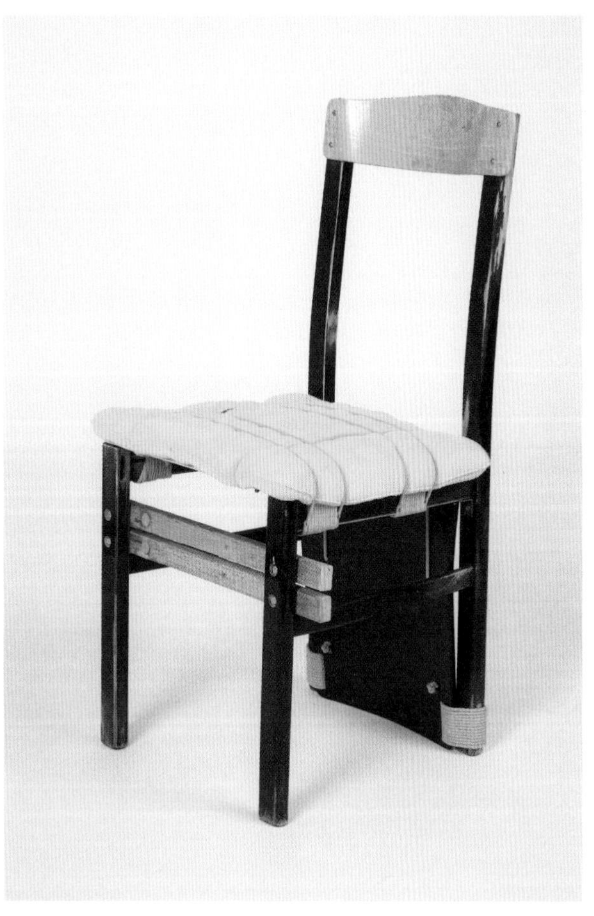

Claudia Clare

Having trained as a painter at Camberwell School of Art in the 1980s, Claudia Clare (1962, Oxford, UK) turned to pottery as a more effective medium to tell the stories she wanted to share. 'The turning surface is sympathetic to an unfolding visual narrative,' she says. 'Pots are our museum pieces and our archaeological and documentary evidence. Their human, cultural and historic associations appeal to me as a feminist artist interested in recording and interpreting women's histories and contemporary lives – feminism that centres women and campaigns against men's violence against them.' But she was also attracted to what many people view as a flaw in pots: they are brittle and fragile – in other words, they break. 'Pots can be broken and they can be rebuilt,' she says. 'That provides a compelling metaphor for the human experience of trauma and survival.'

Having produced works such as *Shattered* (2004–7) and *Remembering Atefeh* (2013) in which she hand-built, broke and then mended pots in order to deploy precisely that metaphor, Clare was approached by women@thewell, a London-based charity supporting women whose lives have been affected by prostitution. The organisation invited her to create work that would undermine some of the misconceptions surrounding the sex trade and focus instead on the lived experience of the women they support, as well as highlighting some of the barriers to getting out of prostitution and rebuilding their lives. 'They asked me to challenge the most popular and prevalent myths – the "Pretty Woman" myth, the idea that "sex-work is work" and the "street vs high-class" prostitute myth. There is no such thing as a "high-class" prostitute; they're all

Claudia Clare with *I'm Not The Criminal*, 2019

the same women,' she says. 'The charity also asked me to focus on surviving the sex trade, rather than living and dying in it.'

For this commission, as for many of her other works, she started by hand-building each pot and painting images on both its inside and outside with slip (coloured liquid clay) as she built it up. 'I often say I only make pots so I've got something to paint on,' she says. 'Doing so gives me two canvases – a broken pot can be rebuilt with pieces left out so the viewer can see the interior images as well as those on the outside.'

Her pots are then fired and broken. She sometimes breaks them in her studio, but more often at a public event, memorial or protest. One particular pot, which in its unbroken state was called *The Invisible Man,* was broken as part of a march against the sex trade in Bradford. 'As well as being a protest, it was also a memorial procession and it ended with a vigil in Centenary Square, during which the names of all the women murdered in prostitution since records began were called out,' explains Clare. 'At the end of a minute's silence, the pot was smashed. Breaking a pot in front of an audience makes me nervous, but it brings the narrative home to the audience more effectively. When I do it at an event with speakers, audience members also recall the words of the speakers better.' Another reason to smash her pots is to express the violence of the sex trade. 'I do not want to hide from it, but I have no desire to reproduce images of sexualised violence against women in pictorial form, so smashing the pots allows me to represent that violence metaphorically,' says Clare.

Fighters and Survivors, 2021

women@thewell, 2019

She then reassembles the broken pots, leaving some shards out, so that the images inside are made visible. She rebuilds each pot – using tape in the first instance – to get a sense of which pieces to omit and what sort of images, if any, to add to the pot. At this stage she uses a paint brush and underglaze colours. Then she dismantles the pot again and glazes the shards. Having learned to repair ceramics in the British Museum's conservation department, she uses conservation-grade adhesive that she gilds with gold, platinum or aluminium leaf to frame the internal images or to emphasise a broken line. 'I see mending and repair as a metaphor for surviving trauma and rebuilding a shattered life,' she says. 'But it also insists on the existence of trauma in the first place, on the need for rebuilding, and on the continuation of vulnerability into the long term. The rebuilt pot will always be vulnerable to further pressure.'

In the case of *women@thewell* (2019, above) – the piece that resulted from the charity's commission – because the images inside depict scenes that the women who shared them (anonymously and consentingly) would rather forget, they are only just visible through narrow cracks. In the case of *The Invisible Man* - renamed *I'm Not The Criminal* in its broken and reassembled state (p. 136) – the negative images are on the exterior, so the images inside are made more clear. The outside of the latter had been painted with 'a burlesque of hideous characters on the sex-trade merry-go-round,' says Clare. 'These are the men who buy sex; men who pay to abuse exploited and prostituted women and girls. One of the reasons these pots are

Detail from *Fighters and Survivors*, 2021

broken and rebuilt is to smash the power and dominance of these men, and to bring out and emphasise the courage and persistence of the women who speak out, "break" the silence, and campaign for change.' The colours inside are therefore lighter and brighter than the exterior colours, so that the interior images – triumphant women free from the sex trade and now fighting it – are clearly visible through the gaps. After the pot was broken, Clare also added a portrait of Fiona Broadfoot – a sex-trade survivor and campaigner for its abolition – on the biggest shard, to ensure her image was complete.

If her work is activism and part of the feminist social justice movement, as Clare emphasises, what does she hope it will achieve? 'I hope to see vastly improved services to prevent girls and women being exploited in the sex trade in the first place, and to help them get out once they have been ensnared. And also a change in the legal settlement from the muddle we have now to one that decriminalises all prostituted persons and criminalises pimps and punters,' she says. 'I also hope to see a far better understanding and provision of trauma-informed support and care for women using mental health and drug and alcohol rehab services.' It is perhaps a lot to ask from a humble pot, but the power of Clare's work is that it starts conversations. 'I showed four pieces in a shop window opposite a café and a hair salon,' she says. 'Two years later, people still talk to me about them and ask questions.'

Pots can be broken and they can be rebuilt. It is a compelling metaphor for the human experience of trauma and survival.

Detail from *February, Cold and Dark*, 2020

Detail from *Brave Face*, 2022

Detail from *Brave Face*, 2022

I'm Not The Criminal, 2019

I do not want to hide from it, but I have no desire to reproduce images of sexualised violence against women by these men in pictorial form, so smashing the pots allows me to represent that violence metaphorically.

Repair as healing

Repair [verb] – to betake oneself, to come together, to go (to a place)[1]

Repair mends and heals, and repair returns us to a place of comfort, nurture or solace. Repair completes us. Repair calls us home.

– John Wackman & Elizabeth Knight[2]

As I stitched a 'secret' message on to the care label of a top I had darned for my sister and patched the knees of her two young sons' trousers, I became unexpectedly emotional. I felt a surge of love for all three of them, combined with guilt for the times I had prioritised other things over spending time with them. I enjoy sewing – I find it calming and grounding – but, by mending their clothes, I realised I was attempting to repair our relationship too.

There are a lot of words in the English language with more than one definition, but the word repair doesn't just have two meanings. According to etymologists, it should actually be two entirely distinct words – *repare* and *repair.* The better-known definition, to mend or to fix, comes from the Latin *reparare*, and should by all rights have retained its original spelling, *repare*. But by happenstance it entered the lexicon at the same time as another very similar word, and the two merged. *Repair*, from the Old French *repairer*, meant and still means to come home, with specific reference to animals returning to a den or lair. (We also talk about 'repairing' to a more comfortable room after a meal.) 'I delight in the way these two meanings intertwine,' write John Wackman and Elizabeth Knight in their book, *Repair Revolution*.[3] 'It is a deepening.' And so do I, because I realised that by making the time to mend those clothes, I was coming home too – to my family.

The extra depth of meaning that this coincidence brings to the word repair is particularly relevant to the role that mending can play in healing ourselves, our relationships and our communities. Think of the words we use to describe mental, emotional and relational injury: we talk about *shattered* confidence, we *break* everything, from hearts and promises to confidentiality, people's worlds *fall apart* when they suffer a loss, and we describe *rips* or *tears* in the social *fabric* of communities. And after that harm has occurred and we need to make good, we turn again to the language of repair: we *patch things up* after an argument, *heal* rifts, *mend* broken hearts and seek *restorative* justice.[4]

But this is more than mere metaphor. 'What I've discovered is that there's a critical link between symptoms of depression and key areas of the brain involved with motivation, pleasure, movement and thought,' says behavioural neuroscience researcher Kelly Lambert. In her book *Lifting Depression*, she argues that the easy rewards of consumer culture just don't light up what she calls the 'effort-driven rewards circuit' in our brains and therefore don't create the conditions for happiness, but that an antidote to depression can be 'generated by doing certain types of physical activities, especially ones that involve your hands, which give us an emotional sense of well-being'.[5] A mindfulness technique commonly recommended for the management of anxiety involves tuning into all five senses in turn, to come into the present moment and the body, drawing attention away from mental ruminations on the past or the future. 'The repairman has to begin every job by getting outside his own head and noticing things, he has to *look* carefully and *listen* to the ailing machine,'[6] writes Matthew Crawford in his book *Shop Class as Soulcraft* (my emphasis), inadvertently positioning repair as the perfect physical activity for mindfulness.

Catching on to these ideas, the UK's Department of Health and Social Care is starting to support a concept called 'social prescribing' instead of, or to supplement, the use of anti-depressants and anti-anxiety medication. Ellie Mosely is a social prescribing link worker for Morrab Surgery in Penzance, Cornwall; as well as referring patients to practical services to help with things like debt and housing, she introduces patients to each other. Although she finds any physical or creative activity can spark conversations and eventually even friendships, which help to alleviate loneliness, anxiety and depression, she does believe there is something special about the metaphor of mending. 'You often use metaphor in therapy,' she says. 'You wouldn't necessarily talk directly about the "damaged" part of somebody, but you might use a metaphor instead to enable their brain to take in the message without getting their defences up.' The act of repair suggests that if a damaged object is worthy of repair and can be functional or beautiful after it's been fixed, then perhaps the person mending it can also heal and see themselves as worthy and beautiful again. 'There's a message that filters into that individual about their own "damage" and their own worthiness, not just in spite of the healing, but because of it,' says Mosely.

Fixing things in community with others only amplifies the effectiveness of repair as a tool for promoting well-being. 'Informal gestures in the [repair] shop relate and bind people emotionally; the power of small gestures is felt too in communal ties,' says Richard Sennett in his book *Together.*[7] Having lost local hubs such as churches, post offices and village pubs, many communities have become fractured, with fewer and fewer people even speaking to their nearest neighbours. Mosely's work brings together people who might not otherwise meet and so rebuilds links and heals fractures. 'The act of mending... profoundly mirrors the brokenness and healing we experience in human relationships and connects us to our sense of individual and social well-being,' write Wackman and Knight.[8] And Janet Gunter found the same thing when she co-founded The Restart Project in 2012. She was not at all surprised by what she describes at the 'mountain of stuff and endless demand for repairs', but what she wasn't expecting was how many volunteers the project would attract. 'So many people really wanted to share their skills,' she says. Many of the volunteers are retired and, with loneliness endemic among older generations in developed countries (according to Age UK, more than a million people over the age of 75 can go for over a month without speaking to a friend, neighbour or family member[9]), volunteering alongside others can be an incredibly powerful remedy. 'Bringing everybody together immediately created this community of repairers,' says Gunter. 'These connections "de-garbage" materials and knowledge,' adds Bridget Harvey (p. 98), co-organiser of a similar London-based initiative, Hackney Fixers.[10] This 'de-garbaging' gives a sense of dignity back to people who might previously have felt their skills were outdated. And it's not just older people who feel alone. In a survey taken even before the Covid pandemic, 88% of 18–24 years olds in Britain reported experiencing loneliness.[11] With social isolation identified by the NHS as a contributing factor in depression, the cross-generational interactions that collaborative repair fosters can only improve well-being. Mending together rebuilds personal well-being, fosters friendship and rebuilds trust in communities.

As well as the physical act of mending, its intent also heals. Globalised consumer culture has distanced us from the people who make the objects we surround ourselves with and created gatekeepers to their repair. When something breaks, what happens next is rarely up to us and that can leave us feeling powerless. A faceless corporation decides if we get a refund or a replacement, rarely offering repair as an option, and they also decide what happens to the broken object we may or may not be asked to return. If online retailers are destroying even perfect returns,[12] it's hard to imagine broken goods getting a second life. There is a growing sense of anger at built-in obsolescence, 'locked' products designed to be impossible to repair, and the inequality that exists because cheaper things break more frequently and are harder to mend – the so-called 'poverty-premium'.[13]

Taking matters into our own hands, literally, and attempting to repair a broken object gives us a sense of agency. Agency is defined in the social sciences as 'the capacity of an individual to... affect change' and 'an expression of autonomy against social institutions, structures, and cultural forces',[14] and it turns us from passive consumers into active citizens. 'Hackney Fixers workshops subvert brokenness into positive, community-led, knowledge-sharing opportunities, giving space for "talking back" and participants' control,' says Harvey.[15] Repair reconnects us to the people who made the objects and engenders respect for their labour. It brings us closer to each other and helps us to feel that we are contributing, even in a tiny way, to a more fair and just society, giving us a sense of purpose. 'A lot of our volunteers are motivated by not just the thrift or the environmental benefits of repair, but by the fundamental unfairness of our current consumer economy,' says Gunter.[16] 'These connections... redefine ownership, choices, values and power,' adds Harvey.[17] 'The focus on repair-making together, even if it turns out to be impossible or needs more materials or time, shows repair to be a key tool for the disenfranchised.'

There's a reason that Linda Brothwell (p. 174) calls her public mending projects Acts of Care. By restoring public benches or shopfront signs, she pays attention to the often-neglected communities in which they exist – likewise Bachor (p. 166) saw a creative way to improve day-to-day life for his local community by filling potholes with mosaics. For Aono Fumiaki (p. 154), whose work uses debris left behind by the 2011 earthquake and resulting tsumani, mending is about rebuilding lives. For Ekta Kaul (p. 144) and Lucy Willow (p. 150) the healing embodied in their work is both deeply personal and also a bid for community connection. Meanwhile social enterprise Goldfinger (p. 160) uses repair as both a metaphor for the healing process of their volunteers and also to teach them valuable skills with which they can give back to their communities. As technology forecaster Alex Pang says, 'Today we tinker with things; tomorrow we will tinker with the world.'[18]

Ekta Kaul

Ekta Kaul

While visiting India to research an upcoming book about *kantha*, London-based artist Ekta Kaul (1977, Hisar, India) visited Kolkata, West Bengal, in the hope of learning more about her maternal grandmother, who had died when Kaul's mother was just nine years old. 'With not much to go on besides the name of the street where she lived 80 years ago, I only found dead ends,' she says. Kaul was able to locate the neighbourhood where she believed her grandmother had lived, but no one in the local community remembered her. To process her disappointment and renewed sense of loss, Kaul turned to art – she hand-embroiders maps that explore themes of place, history and belonging. 'Having been unable to find my grandmother in Kolkata, I tried to find her through my practice,' she says. 'I approach repair as an act of healing. To stitch is to mend feelings of loss, to process emotions, to hold on to memories and to create new connections with what I hold precious. *Threads of Connection* maps the neighbourhoods of Kolkata that my grandmother would have known in her childhood. Now that I'm back in London, I can imagine her walking along the Hooghly river as I walk along the Thames.'

The 'ground cloth' (background fabric) was made by piecing together white, cream and beige offcuts from clothing brand Toast with remnants from Kaul's own studio, using tiny, precise, white stitches. Toast commissioned the work for *Eternally Yours* (2022), an exhibition about mending and repair at London's Somerset House. 'I created the ground cloth like a collage, building it up slowly with multiple layers of fabric,' says Kaul. 'Then I hand-stitched the map on to this ground cloth. This way of working allows for serendipity and play. The vocabulary of stitches I use is inspired by *kantha* and traditional mending techniques, like darning stitches. *Kantha*, which originates in Bengal and gives new life to old cloth, seemed a fitting segue into exploring our lost connection.' Poignantly, the part of the map where Kaul believes her grandmother lived 80 years ago is left blank – the place that she hoped would spill its secrets during her trip: still empty.

Kaul grew up in the north of India, the daughter of entomologists (insect scientists). 'They were passionate advocates for conserving the planet's precious resources and its biodiversity, and so they championed repair and creative reuse,' she says. 'Respect for materials and care for our possessions were ingrained in us from early childhood. My mother unravelled jumpers we had outgrown to create new ones, invented recipes to reuse leftovers, and darned holes with joyful motifs, while my dad would always remind us of the farmers who worked so hard in the fields for the food on our table.' In fact, it was only when Kaul came to the UK to study for her master's in textiles at Heriot-Watt University in Edinburgh, and heard terms like 'slow cooking' or 'seasonal eating', that she realised that this respect for natural resources was the exception rather than the norm elsewhere in the world – something that needed a name. 'The ethos of repair, reuse and recycling is so deeply rooted in the Indian way of life that you almost don't notice it,' she says. 'And there is an entire ecosystem to support that, so the instinct is never to throw away, but to conserve and re-imagine. Repair shops, which are everywhere, mend everything from zippers to kitchen appliances. And recycling is incentivised – you can exchange old saris for new vessels, and old newspapers and glass bottles for cash.'

Kaul came to Edinburgh to continue her exploration into what she calls the 'poetics of damage' following her undergraduate apparel and textiles degree at the National Institute of Design (NID) in Ahmedabad – India's premier design school – where she had connected the dots between academic teachings on circular practices and eco-design and her childhood experiences. 'I've been interested in textiles for as long as I can remember,' she says. 'Growing up in India, I fell in love with the beautiful handmade textiles I was surrounded by – be it my mum's handwoven saris and shawls or vibrant rugs and *kantha* quilts at home. My earliest teachers were my mother and my paternal grandmother. My grandmother taught me how to stitch *gudri* quilts using multiple layers of discarded cloth.' (Similar to *kantha*, quilts made by stitching layers of cast-off cloth are known as *gudri* in north India, and Kaul

Kantha, which originates in Bengal and gives new life to old cloth, seemed a fitting segue into exploring our lost connection.

uses these materials and techniques to this day.) 'Textiles form an important element of the material culture of India – they are part of so many rituals and rites of passage,' she says. 'To me, cloth is deeply emotive. It holds memories and meaning, so I chose it as the medium to express my ideas in.'

Kaul's work invites people to think of stitching as a transformative act of emotional repair – and so she often invites them to take part, running workshops and co-creating artworks with members of the public. While *Threads of Connection* (pp. 147 and 148) sought to repair a personal sense of loss, *Portrait of Place* (p. 149) was a participatory art project conceived to bring together a diverse local community that felt it had no connection with Gunnersbury Park Museum in west London, which commissioned the ten-week participatory project and resulting artwork. Kaul worked with two local groups: the Deaf and Hard of Hearing Women's Group in Ealing; and Heston West Big Local in Hounslow, an intergenerational group of people with Middle Eastern, South Asian, African and European heritage. She took the groups foraging in the museum's gardens and identified plants and trees that are not indigenous to the UK, using the leaves to directly print the border of the artwork. Within the border, the two groups co-created a map that reflected *their* Gunnersbury. Kaul embroidered the name of every participant on to the final piece, which is now on permanent display at the museum. One participant told her: 'I would have never come here before, but now I would love to bring my friends, because my name is on there.' By enabling them to define their locality and by naming them as authors of its image, she empowered them to reclaim ownership.

'As a contemporary artist, I see my role as a catalyst for change, and very much part of the wider environmental movement,' says Kaul. 'By acquainting people – especially those in the Global North – with traditional stitch practices such as *kantha* that are rooted in sustainability, and by sharing creative processes and diverse creative expressions, I hope I can bring a change in perspectives and practices. Hand-stitch is a mindful, healing act. The nature of the process is slow and meditative. When stitching is done collectively, it allows for conversation to flow and stories to be shared easily. For centuries, men and women have stitched in groups to alleviate isolation, to share stories and to feel connected to their neighbours and community. My hope for the future is that reparative stitch practices will be adopted widely as acts of healing for ourselves and for the environment.'

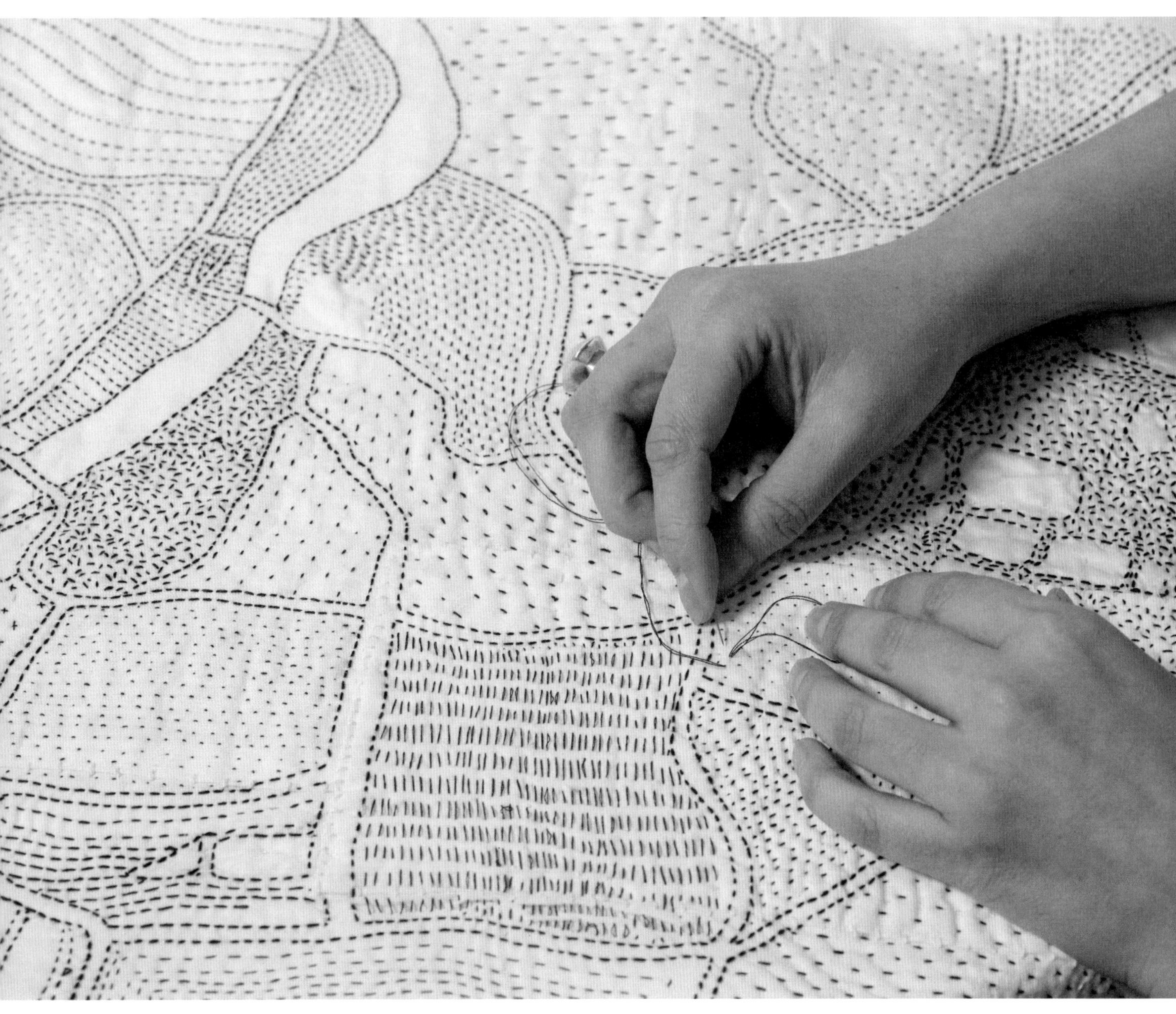

Ekta Kaul embroidering *Threads of Connection*

Threads of Connection, 2022

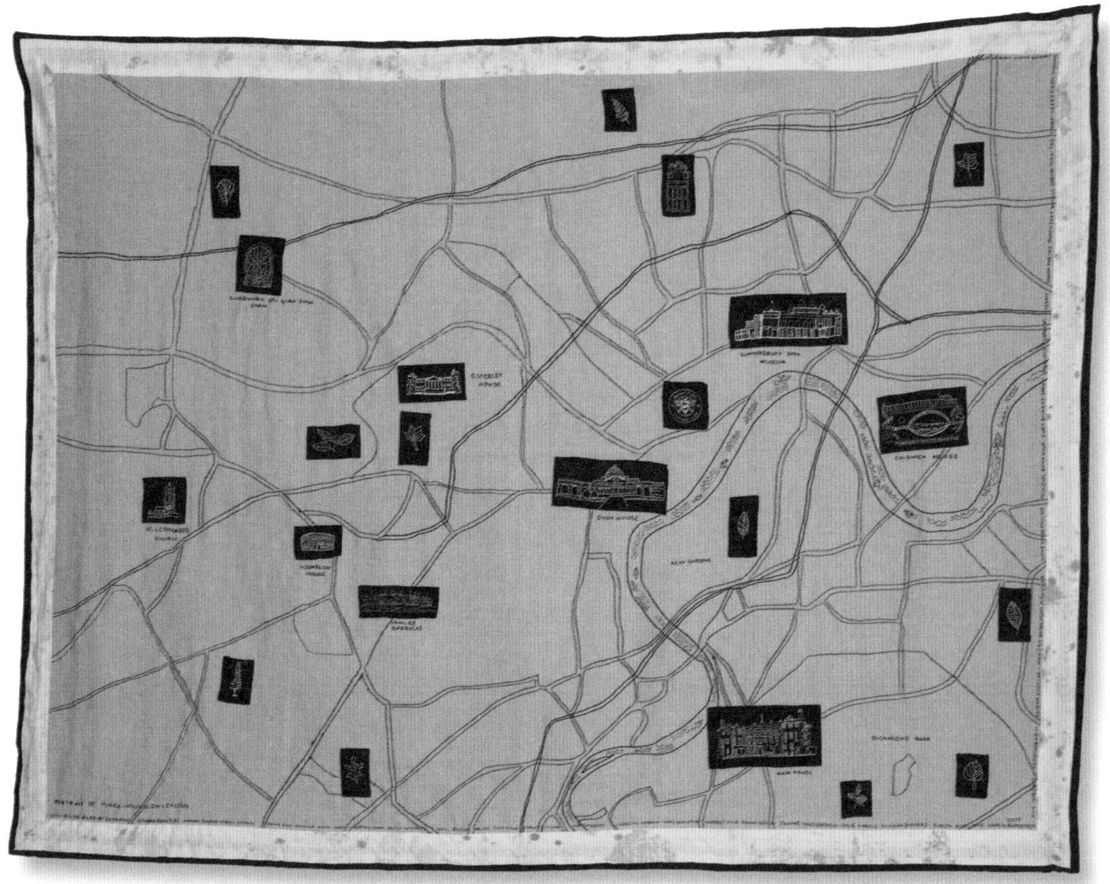

Portrait of Place – Hounslow & Ealing, 2019

Lucy Willow

Lucy Willow

If you were in Cornwall in November 2022, you might have found yourself in Penryn, near Falmouth. If you did, there is a relatively high chance you would have passed some time ambling along Commercial Road, perhaps browsing a few shops, stopping for a coffee. You might even have popped your head into Grays Wharf – a small but perfectly formed gallery and workshop space for local artists. And if you did that, there is no question that what you saw would have stopped you in your tracks. Because *Drawn from the Well* (pp. 152–153)– an exhibition created and curated by Lucy Willow (1967, Whitstable, Kent) as an outcome of a nine-month residency at CAST in nearby Helston – had that effect. The works were made in response to an ancient well that Willow discovered on the boundary line of a memorial garden for her late son, Jack Perry, whom she lost in 2006 when he was nearly 16. (There is something quietly devastating about the fact that Willow describes Jack not as 15 when he died, but as 'nearly 16'.) The deep black charcoal drawings on the walls and the broken porcelain ceramic forms across the floor are hauntingly beautiful, but it is the stitched textile sculptures that provide the gut-punch – the connection to whatever raw and tender grief you carry within your own internal landscape.

Made from Jack's clothes and schoolbooks, the abstract forms evoke umbilical cords tumbling out of wombs. 'When I first started thinking about the well, I thought about the idea of an umbilical cord that could go down into a space that can connect you with something otherworldly or linked with the dead,' says Willow. 'I'm always looking at ways that, in a metaphorical or symbolic sense, we can communicate with the dead, because those relationships continue – I still feel as if I'm a mother to Jack, to a child who isn't here anymore.' The umbilical cords feature heavy stitches down one side – an attempt to repair what has been lost. 'The mending is really rough and raw, very much about stitching something together in a very visible way, in a very bodily way,' she says. 'These textile pieces tend to get left out of exhibitions when other people curate them – there's something that is undesirable, that we don't want to confront. I can and do make things that are aesthetically easy to live with. And then there are these pieces, that really aren't as easy to live in relationship with.'

But death isn't easy to live in relationship with either, and that's what Willow's work explores. 'A lot of my work is about our relationship with grief, which is a relationship with the love I still have for Jack,' she says. 'The idea that I didn't know where this black space in the garden ended became symbolic of my experience of grief – it's never-ending, it goes down and down and down, further into layers and layers.' Willow spent a lot of time just sitting in the ancient well – which she describes as 'a cave with steps leading down into a deep, dark space' – thinking and writing. 'I love exploring the narrative of a space through creative writing, so I spent lots of time in there, just writing,' she explains. 'And then, feeling as if I was looking down into this dark – this depth, the idea of a symbolic womb space emerged, and I started to wonder what would happen if I started excavating that place.'

The first works Willow made were a series of charcoal drawings through a process she imagined was similar to scrying (sometimes explained as divination) – the idea of the artist as a medium who can communicate with the unseen. 'I'm not sure what the right word is, because I'm not really mystical or spiritual, but there's a space you can connect to when making work, and images can be drawn from that,' she says. 'So, it's working with an intuitive knowledge about a space, and making drawings from that knowledge.' The drawings started to look like ultrasound scans, which she didn't expect. 'They look like an empty womb space,' she says. Next came the porcelain fragments. 'They feel as if they were drawn up from this well space,' she says. 'When they're fired, they look like skin and bone and they tell a story of grief because they're broken, they're fragmented, they're lying on the floor.'

But these are not the pieces Willow can find herself in. 'The charcoal and porcelain pieces are easy to live with, but I feel I'm invisible in that work. But the textile pieces – they are about tearing, ripping, stabbing, breaking. I'm connected to the cloth, to the materials

Drawn from the Well, 2022. Installation view with charcoal drawing

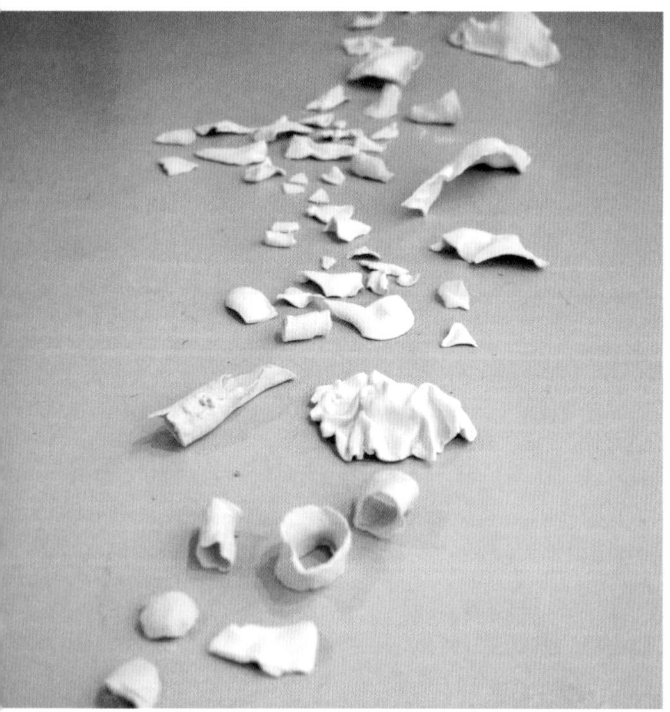

Magnetic Field, 2022. Broken porcelain ceramics

that I'm using, and it really does feel as if I'm stitching something bodily together – they've really visceral. Parental grief is so difficult for people to hold the space for, so you find that you just can't talk about the details of that experience. In these pieces is the anger, the rawness, the loss that I haven't been able to share – there is a literal sense of "spilling my guts". But there's also something powerful about the mending, the binding and the stitching. I'm not trying to do it invisibly – I'm trying to show the visible marks of how I'm putting myself back together again. So that feels ritualistic; that feels really important in my work.'

The pieces Willow created as part of her CAST residency and the resulting exhibition at Grays Wharf are just one example of a broad and diverse body of work that holds space for communities to come together, to share their own stories and to think and reflect. 'I really hope that I carry on being invited to make work of this sort,' she says. 'My work often prompts people to reflect on what's lost, on what's broken, on their own grief – and it's so important that there are spaces quiet enough for people to contemplate these things. It's so rare, isn't it, that you really sit down and listen to somebody's story?' While working recently with 13-year-old pupils in a school, Willow talked to them about the *Drawn from the Well* projects. One of the boys said, 'Your work is so sad, but life is sad.' The discussion that comment opened up felt important: 'We had this amazing conversation – at a 13-year-old level – of how sad feelings could be put into making art,' she says. 'If you've got to live through what we're all facing in the world today, there is so much grief. I can't say I'm changing the world, but my hope is to continue making spaces where we get to reflect on that.'

Inside Out, 2022. Porcelain object with textile interior

My work often prompts people to reflect on what's lost, on what's broken, on their own grief – and it's so important that there are spaces quiet enough for people to contemplate these things.

Aono Fumiaki

Aono Fumiaki with *The SHINDEN that used to be in my town: Restoration of Yagiyama Koejiyama Shrine*, 2000–19

In 1991, Aono Fumiaki (1968, Sendai City, Japan) was preparing for his graduate project at Miyagi University of Education. Having grown up in the Tohoku region of northern Japan – a region rich in nature – he had decided to make art inspired by his favourite forest. However, partway through his research and fieldwork, the woodland was cut down to make way for a park. 'I was so shocked that I could no longer make forest-themed productions,' he says. 'I thought hard about what to do. It seemed more important to recreate the original trees than to create something new. I tried to regenerate the forest by collecting and tying the cut trees together. Instead of creating new and different works, I tried to recreate what had been lost. Instead of trying to express myself in a unique way, I tried to get directly involved with the severed tree in front

Umi-no-kazuko: Restoration of the Sato clothing store swept away by the tsunami in Kuwagasaki, Miyako, Iwate prefecture, 2019

of me, the concrete reality. I tried to repair the reality I faced.'

In the 20 years that followed, Aono became known for assemblages and sculptures made from damaged and discarded objects such as pieces of torn cloth, pages of newspapers and broken signboards that he repaired, reshaped and reformed. Then in 2011, a catastrophic earthquake (the strongest ever recorded in Japan) and tsunami struck the Tohoku region and gave new meaning to his artistic practice. The tsunami washed away parts of Aono's studio and his wife's family home and devastated much of the local community. He soon began picking up the pieces – literally as well as metaphorically. 'The problem was not the disaster,' he said at the time. 'It was how we were going to rebuild our lives afresh. After the earthquake and tsunami, what matters more is the restoration of meaning rather than form.' Aono set about gathering the debris scattered by the tsunami, ranging from small everyday objects such as plastic bottles, wooden boxes and books to items as large and iconic as a red Coca-Cola signboard. He then began to put them back together.

He covered a wooden table with the lino he had torn from the site where his parents-in-law's house once stood, because 'I wanted to restore the lost life by adding broken objects to furniture we are using now, because people should continue to live despite the tragic incident.' He piled up books, wooden boxes and a discarded plastic bottle he had collected on the streets of Yuriage, Miyagi prefecture, to create an installation resembling a Buddhist stone pagoda. It represents, he says, a 'prayer for the souls lost in the tsunami'. At the 2013 Aichi Triennale, Aono showed a destroyed boat from the tsunami-stricken city of Ishinomaki (p. 158). He explained that the process of restoring it echoed 'how we are rebuilding our broken lives', adding: 'The only thing an artist [can do in a disaster such as this] is to create art every day and show what's right in life through my work.'

Aono prefers to use simple repair techniques that anyone could perform, rather than specialist methods. He changes the collected pieces as little as possible, his interventions limited to 'filling the missing shapes with [his] imagination', because he wants both the damage and repair to remain visible; he wants his work to bear witness to both the tragic events of 2011 and the resilience of the communities affected in the recovery effort afterwards. 'Self-restoration does not require artifice to cover up the action, since the action itself is important,' he says. 'While repairing the missing parts of the things we have found – cars, people and houses – we will be able to imagine how they existed, how they were destroyed, and how they could be in the future.' Introducing 'ready-made' forms such as furniture, boxes and books creates juxtapositions he finds interesting. 'I am interested in the intersection of things from different worlds, such as the unknown waste that I have picked up and the materials that are familiar to me in my daily life,' he says. 'The old part and the new part are combined.'

Despite having felt like a lone voice for much of his 30-year career, he believes things are starting to change. 'When I started this "repair" work 30 years ago, I was always alone,' he says. 'After the 2011 earthquake and tsunami, people began to understand it little by little. I believe that "restoration and regeneration" are based on a common awareness of issues at this time when human civilisation is at a turning point. It will not end with mere recycling and ecological activities, but will give us significance and vitality.'

While repairing the missing parts of the things we have found – cars, people and houses – we will be able to imagine how they existed, how they were destroyed, and how they could be in the future.

Restoration of a red signboard collected in Ishinomaki, Miyagi Japan, after the great East Japan earthquake and tsunami, 2013

The problem was not the disaster. It was how we were going to rebuild our lives afresh.

Restoration of a boat collected in Ishinomaki, Miyagi, Japan, after the great East Japan earthquake and tsunami, 2012

Restoration of a green cassette tape in Yuriage, Natori, Miyagi, Japan, after the great East Japan earthquake and tsunami, 2012

Restoration of a TV remote control collected in Yuriage, Natori, Miyagi, Japan, after the great East Japan earthquake and tsunami, 2014

Marie Cudennec Carlisle & Daniele Barco

Marie Cudennec Carlisle, Goldfinger CEO and co-founder

The Royal Borough of Kensington and Chelsea is one of London's most inequitable boroughs. It has the highest income gap between rich and poor[1] in the capital, and, in the area around Golborne Road, life expectancy can vary by as much as 17 years.[2] In a borough in which some houses can sell for more than £10 million, two-thirds of children live in overcrowded homes.[3] 'With our social enterprise mission, it was a very strategic decision to be here,' says Goldfinger co-founder Marie Cudennec Carlisle (1987, Singapore). 'This is a very divided community, and we want to be a bridge.' Nestled at the bottom of the iconic – and controversial – Trellick Tower (hence the organisation's name – architect Erno Goldfinger designed the tower), Goldfinger takes a three-pronged approach to repairing fractures within the community. The Goldfinger Academy teaches

Bespoke Goldfinger dining tables in Panella

woodworking skills to school children as well as marginalised young people, including young offenders and those excluded from mainstream education, and also offers Soulcraft workshops to the public, with free spaces for those on low income in the area. The People's Kitchen tackles both food waste and social isolation by providing vulnerable local residents with restaurant-quality meals made from surplus food. And then there's the woodwork and joinery workshop, where highly skilled craftspeople are literally turning trash into treasure to fund the whole operation. Taking wood that is often destined for landfill, chippings or use as fuel – some of it from trees felled for development or safety reasons within London – they design and craft bespoke furniture and homeware for homes and high-end businesses, ranging from hotels and cafés to shops and offices.

'Rather than passing like ships in the night, the two sides of this community actually have a lot to contribute to one another,' says Cudennec Carlisle. 'We wanted to be located in an area where people need the engagement and employment opportunities we can offer, but also close enough to an affluent population, so they can come and buy from us – that's very much at the core of everything we do at Goldfinger.'

The Ayrton collection (pp. 164–165) is a case in point. Launched during London Craft Week in 2021, the original limited-edition desk, bench, chair and side table were designed and made by Goldfinger's Daniele Barco (1988, Rome, Italy) from reclaimed teak donated by Imperial College London after it had been stripped out of their science labs in a refurbishment. This was paired with reclaimed Douglas fir from another project. 'When we went to look at the material, we found massive solid teak desks, which meant long runs – two and a half metres at a time – of solid wood,' says Barco. 'So, the design of the collection was inspired by the desire to process that wood as little as possible and by the colour contrast between the teak and the fir.' Decades of use had resulted in quite a lot of surface damage from chemicals and burns, but once sanded, the teak was in incredibly good condition. 'Everyone talks about innovation, but the more I see it, the more I think we're actually just going back to how things were. We need to revert back to old ways of mending and repairing and using resources to their full potential,' says Cudennec Carlisle. 'If we can save wood from being chipped or burned, and instead use craft and creativity to elevate it into something that will last for another 200 years – with all that captured carbon – that's got to be more sustainable than importing virgin wood. It's really just pushing the boundaries of what the new normal should be. There are solutions: you just have to care enough and be willing to work hard enough to make them happen.'

Daniele Barco, lead designer maker at Goldfinger

Everyone talks about innovation, but we need to revert back to old ways of mending and repairing and using resources to their full potential.

If wood is donated in less usable pieces, Barco employs traditional patchwork techniques to connect smaller pieces together or adds 'bow-ties' to repair and stabilise cracks. 'Wood expands and contracts depending on the moisture content in the air, so a bow-tie is a really simple and visually descriptive way to stabilise a crack,' he says. 'A crack can be seen as a defect, but this technique turns it into a feature.'

Alongside the formal mending activities at the workshop, an informal repair service has also emerged, purely by accident. 'One day a guy came in with a broken chair,' says Barco. 'I glued it back together in less than ten minutes. He wanted to pay us, but I just asked him to make a donation to the People's Kitchen. That happens a couple of times a month now, which is a really interesting development. It's not something we promote, but people know we make furniture, so I guess they figure we can mend it too.'

Whether it's the formal apprenticeship programme or an informal favour for a local resident, the most healing thing Goldfinger has done for the local community is not only to redistribute wealth, but to create a space where people feel welcome no matter which end of the income spectrum they come from. At the launch party for the Ayrton collection, a fundraising auction demonstrated the wealth and generosity of Goldfinger's supporters, who rubbed shoulders with life-long residents of Trellick Tower and regular participants in those Soulcraft workshops. As Barco puts it, 'We bring people together by bringing them together – it's as simple as that.'

Social and economic inequality is by no means unique to London, and Cudennec Carlisle believes there is potential for Goldfinger's approach to be replicated elsewhere in the world. 'We're starting to see that there's a real appetite for our products, our philosophy, our way of making, and our way of seeing the world,' she says. 'What we do could be applied in France, it could be applied in the US, in Spain, in Italy, in Portugal... As we're starting to get more demand from those geographies, we're looking at ways that we can partner with local makers and localise the supply chain and production process, rather than reinventing the whole thing. I would love to develop a global design community that is socially minded, with the same levels of quality and aesthetics – that's what's really exciting me right now.'

1 www.trustforlondon.org.uk/news/new-analysis-poverty-kensington-chelsea-shows-big-divides-between-rich-andpoor/
2 *Poverty and Prosperity in Kensington + Chelsea*, a WPI Economics report for The Kensington + Chelsea Foundation, November 2021.
3 See note 2.

The Ayrton collection

Detail of the Ayrton side table and Ayrton chair

It was a very strategic decision to be here. This is a very divided community, and we want to be a bridge.

Bachor

'I've got a few good cop stories,' says mosaic artist Jim Bachor (1964, Dearborn, Michigan, US) with a mischievous smile. 'My favourite one happened when I was installing a piece of my work and I could feel the heat of a car pulling up. Without looking up, I said to my assistant, "Is that a cop?" He said "Yeah" and I thought "Oh shit". I stood up and turned around just as he was getting out of the car. "Are you that pothole guy?" he said. I nodded. His response? "That's so fucking cool."'

Bachor doesn't make a habit of attracting police attention, but neither is he quite sure if what he does is entirely legal. He repairs potholes. But instead of using traditional asphalt, he creates complex mosaic artworks that, unlike asphalt, will stand the test of time. 'I can pinpoint the sentence that changed the course of my life,' he says. 'I was in Pompeii and a tour guide pointed out a mosaic in the floor. He said, "Marble and glass don't fade, so this looks exactly the way the artist intended it to 2,000 years ago." Nothing's permanent in this world, but the idea of creating art with that sort of staying power blew me away.'

After a tour of Paris, London and Rome that he reluctantly took at the insistence of a friend, Bachor got hooked on ancient history and eventually returned to Ravenna, near Venice, Italy, to learn the traditional 'direct method' of mosaic making. He creates his designs – which reference popular culture to contrast with his ancient technique – in Photoshop, transfers a pencil outline on to modelling clay and then sets pieces of cut marble and coloured glass into the clay. He attaches a cheesecloth to the top using 'kids' school glue', so that he can lift the whole piece on to a board. He then lowers it into the wet cement, sprays water on to the cloth to release the glue and gently teases the cloth off to reveal the final in-situ design.

It's the in-situ part that makes these works really interesting, because, surrounded by a few traffic cones and wearing a high-vis vest, Bachor is conducting this process on cement he has poured into potholes. 'There was a pothole outside our house that just refused to stay fixed,' he says. 'In the end, I got so frustrated that I decided to do something about it. I liked the idea of repairing this seemingly unsolvable problem with this very durable artform I had become so passionate about.' Tapping into branding experience from his previous career in advertising, he created a logo-inspired design that identified the pothole as an 'authentic Chicago pothole' featuring the iconic city flag. He snuck out under the cover of darkness and installed the piece one night in May 2013.

He carried on filling potholes across the city but didn't want to jeopardise his fledgling career as a mosaic artist – he'd just won a big commission for a mural in a train station – so he kept his work quiet. However, a friend didn't quite get the memo and started emailing pictures of his work to newspapers and local television stations. 'I guess everybody hates potholes and, especially early on, I would depict things that everyone loves, like ice cream, or junk food or flowers,' he says. 'People loved them.'

Bachor in his studio, 2020

This is not a pothole. Anymore., 2021. A multi-piece installation just west of downtown Chicago

Installing *Master Pieces 2*, from a series based on masterworks from the permanent collection of the Art Institute of Chicago, 2022

Apart from the New York Department of Transportation, that is. In 2018, he spent nine days working in the city after a successful crowd-funding campaign and having engaged the services of a 'pothole scout'. The project garnered media attention and one journalist asked him to share the locations of the artworks, which she duly published, contacting the city authorities for comment. The comment came back and it wasn't good. 'We don't like it,' said a spokesperson. 'They're a distraction to drivers. We're taking them out.' Before he'd even returned from his trip to New York, he got a message from someone who had gone out to see them and found nothing more than potholes and a few pieces of broken marble. These days, Bachor is a little more coy about the location of new pieces, posting clues on his website and leaving a prize for whoever finds them first. He says the rewards always get found within 20 minutes, and, thankfully, as far as he knows, no more of his installations have been removed since the New York incident.

So, why does Bachor think his potholes hold such appeal? 'There is that fun juxtaposition of somebody walking or driving down the street and discovering this "Easter egg" in the real world,' he says, highlighting the pleasure of stumbling on a moment of unexpected joy and colour in the otherwise routine progression of day-to-day city life.

There is a theory (popularised in 1982 by social scientists James Q Wilson and George L Kelling, in an article entitled 'Broken Windows' in *The Atlantic*)[1] that visible signs of misdemeanour and civil disobedience create an environment that encourages

Installing *Pb&j* in Chicago's West Loop neighbourhood, 2021

further disorder, eventually leading to a rise in serious crime. Although this theory has undoubtedly been misapplied, leading to 'zero tolerance' stop and search policies that disproportionally affect young Black men, and crime rates are certainly due to a more complex combination of demographic and socio-economic factors, there are examples of projects where tackling seemingly small issues has led to wider community benefits. Eric Klinenberg cites two case studies in his 2018 book *Palaces for the People*[2], in which community gardens planted in burnt-out buildings and vacant lots are helping to improve access to fresh food, lower city temperatures and even reduce gun crime. A review of the book in *Booklist* concluded, 'If America appears fractured at the national level, it can be mended at the local one.'[3]

Bachor's work is a perfect example of the local-level fix in action, but it's not part of some deliberate urban regeneration agenda – or, at least, it wasn't supposed to be. 'It didn't start as a societal project, it's just kind of evolved,' he says. 'I just saw an opportunity to fix some potholes – and now that I have the luxury of having a little bit of microphone, I take advantage of that on occasion. Big protests come and go, but my little pieces of art continue to be there quietly, in their own 24/7 art galleries.'

1 https://www.theatlantic.com/magazine/archive/1982/03/broken-windows/304465/
2 https://www.psychologytoday.com/us/blog/going-beyond-intelligence/202003/palaces-the-people
3 See note 2.

Bachor finishing the installation of *Bouquet* in New York's Chelsea neighbourhood, 2018

It didn't start as a societal project, it's just kind of evolved.

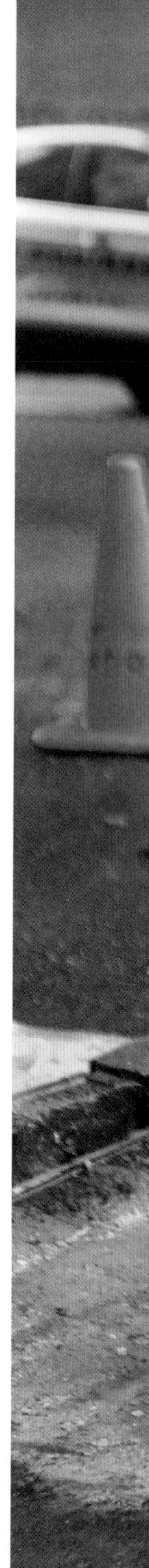

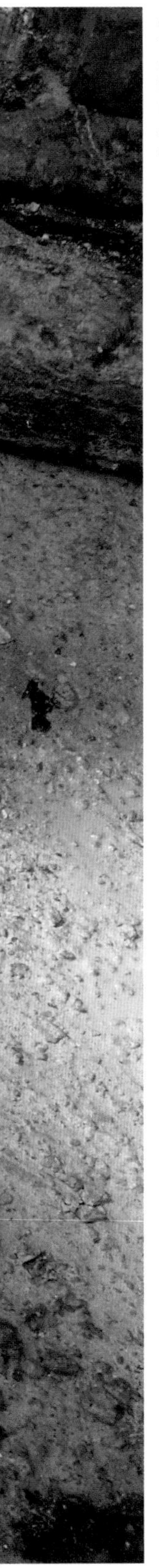

Dead Pigeon was part of a five-piece series called *Vermin of New York*. This particular installation was done in Brooklyn in 2018. The entire series was pulled up within a week by the authorities

I liked the idea of repairing this seemingly unsolvable problem with this very durable artform I had become so passionate about.

Linda Brothwell

Linda Brothwell

Acts of Care is a self-initiated project that runs through everything Bristol-based artist Linda Brothwell (1981, Nottingham, UK) does. She travels all over the world, learning skills from artisans and craftspeople, understanding how these techniques could contribute to local communities and then making all the tools she needs to apply her new-found skills to a different context, usually in the public realm. If that sounds complex, it is. 'There are three main parts to my process,' she says. 'One of them is research, and the documentation of that. Then there is the toolmaking, which results in tools designed specifically for the tasks that I have invented – usually a new combination of material, technique and location. And then there's the public intervention artwork – and they all have to happen at the same time.' But it's also overwhelmingly simple – having

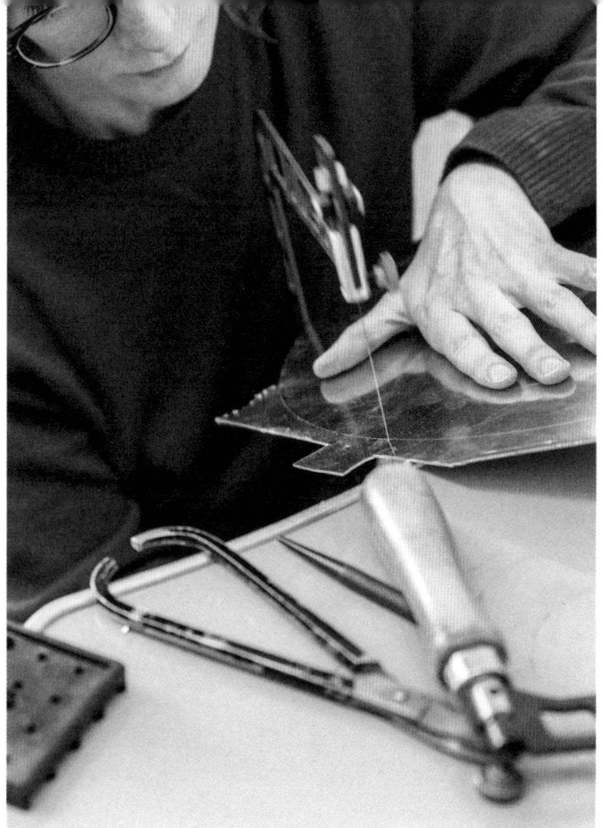

grown up on a farm in Nottinghamshire, improvising tools and techniques to solve problems and repair damage comes naturally to Brothwell. 'When I was growing up, using tools, working outdoors, using my hands and a certain resourcefulness when it comes to damage and repair were all very normal,' she says. 'And I studied jewellery and metalwork in Sheffield, where working with steel and making tools was a normal part of the course – I just took hold of that with both hands and ran with it.'

In 2009, Brothwell was commissioned by the British Council to create a new work in Lisbon as an 'ally to the city', while studying for her master's at the Royal College of Art. She had been surreptitiously darning and embroidering the upholstered seats on the London Underground network prior to this, and went with the idea that there might be a similar opportunity on Lisbon's trams. However, what she noticed was the state of disrepair of Lisbon's wooden public benches, especially outside the tourist areas. While she was in the city, she visited and fell in love with a traditional wood inlay workshop. 'The people there were incredibly talented, so I decided that I wanted to learn wood inlay,' she says. With a background in woodwork, she was confident she could get up to speed quickly enough to make a positive impact, so she planned a six-week return trip to Lisbon during which she documented damaged benches, learned the skills with which she would repair them, and created her public art pieces. 'I wanted to work with what was already there and to fix it,' she says. 'I wanted to create this act of care, this act of community, and repair something that was

Letter A from *Acts of Care: Lost Letters of Liverpool*, 2015

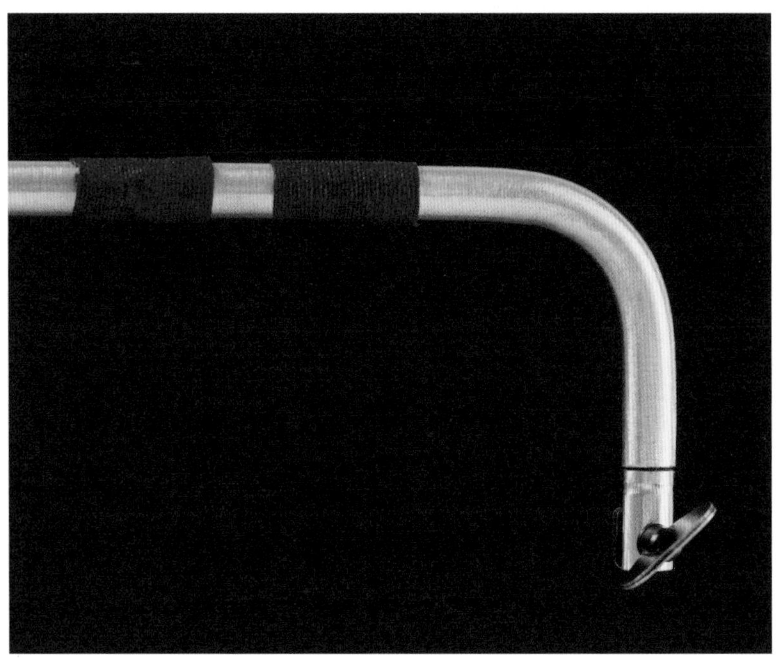

Piercing Saw from *Acts of Care: Lost Letters of Liverpool*, 2015

damaged or broken, to use my skills in a way that I considered to be a positive addition to the city.' The inlay workshop that captured her imagination was attached to the Ricardo do Espírito Santo Silva Foundation, and the technique she learned was inspired by traditional 19th-century 'Dona Maria' designs taken from the very opulent furniture in the museum's collection. Ordinary benches were given an ornate upgrade (pp. 178–179) as Brothwell and her new friends from the workshop replaced the broken slats at night. 'I wanted to share these beautiful designs – which are usually only found in very wealthy homes or in museums – with everybody,' she explains. She is currently working on another iteration in Bristol, to thank the city in which she lives and works, where years of austerity have taken their toll on public spaces.

Three years later, Brothwell found herself exploring another city and once again wondering how she might be useful. She had been commissioned by Liverpool's Fact Gallery and the Crafts Council to create what would become *Acts of Care: Lost Letters of Liverpool* (2015). Exploring the northern English city, she asked herself: 'Where can I put my skills and my thinking and my techniques to use? How can I weave in stories of people and craft and heritage and skills into people's everyday lives to create delight or a new way of thinking?' She noticed that the signage of many public-facing buildings – such as off-licences, bingo halls and libraries – was missing one or more letters. At the time, there was a lot of negative feeling towards, and even hate crimes against, eastern Europeans in Liverpool, so she chose to work with members of the city's Polish community to explore a traditional paper-cutting technique called *wycinanki*. 'I knew that by working with this community, I would find rich and beautiful techniques and skills,' she says. She developed an alphabet and hand-cut highly decorative letters from brass to replace the missing ones all over the city. She made all the tools she needed, from big saws for large pieces of brass, to punches for the decorative cuts and the chasing boards that enable three-dimensionality, all of which were exhibited at Fact Gallery alongside a publication to document the project. 'For all my Acts of Care projects, there will always be a public part – which is the artwork in a public space – which anybody can see whether they feel comfortable in a gallery or not,' she says. 'And simultaneously, there will be tools in an exhibition as well as a newspaper or video. So, the things that I do in public space are often a gift to the city and they stay there permanently. And then the tools and publication are just there for the exhibition.'

Brothwell pays such attention to tools because she believes they are essential to repair. 'Working with repair passes on and preserves skills, because you are becoming a custodian of that object and you need to understand how it was made,' she says. 'But you also need to know how to use – and make – the tools.' She likens the number of specific tools required for certain jobs to biodiversity and the fact that each species – or tool – has a role to play in a complex ecosystem, in this case communities and heritage craft skills. 'It feels like I'm talking about birds or insects, but the number of different types of something such as a hammer is incredibly important because it shows the specificity of tool use within heritage crafts, and that speaks of care, comfort and doing something for long enough to master a skill.'

Chasing Hammer from *Acts of Care: Lost Letters of Liverpool*, 2015

Acts of Care: Bench Repair Project in Lisbon, 2009. Commissioned by Clare Cumberlidge and the British Council for the British Pavilion EXD Biennial (above, below and opposite)

I wandered around the city and thought, where can I be useful?

Acts of Care: Lost Letters of Liverpool, 2015. Commissioned by the Crafts Council and Liverpool's Fact Gallery (above and opposite)

When I was growing up, a certain resourcefulness when it comes to damage and repair was very normal.

HEAD
2015

Regeneration as repair

Regeneration [noun] – the act of improving a place or system, especially by making it more active or successful; the act of something growing or being grown again[1]

The practice of forestry may be changing, but I am unaware of any instances where proficiency in the arts is sought as a professional qualification by timber companies or schools of forestry. Perhaps that is what we need. Artists as foresters.

– Franz Dolp[2]

So far, this book has considered the mending and repair of objects, of the things we have made from the resources we have already taken from the Earth. These acts fulfil the second tenet of the circular economy, as defined by the Ellen MacArthur Foundation: to keep materials and objects in use.[3] They enable us, as humans, to do less harm, because by keeping things in use we avoid replacing them, and therefore we avoid taking more of our planet's resources and using more greenhouse gas-emitting energy to make more things. The more we can slow the replacement cycle, the less damage we do. But in almost two centuries since the Industrial Revolution, we have taken so much, and done so much harm, that it is no longer enough to simply slow down. The third tenet of the circular economy is to restore natural systems, and in fact the Ellen MacArthur Foundation defines the circular economy as 'an industrial economy that is restorative or regenerative by value and design'.[4] It is clear, that to repair the damage we have done to the planet, we need to start actively doing good.

The word 'regeneration' comes from the Old French *regeneracion* (Modern French: *régénération*) and the Late Latin *regenerationem*: a being born again, a make over, or to generate, bring forth, beget or produce again. It originally had spiritual connotations associated with resurrection.[5] There is a sense then, in the environmental context, of another chance or a 'do-over' – the opportunity to mend our relationship with the natural world, and it is in this context that regeneration is included in this book as a form of repair.

Aldo Leopold set out his 'land ethic' in *A Sand Country Almanac* in 1949, stating that 'a thing is right when it tends to preserve the integrity, stability and beauty of the biotic community. It is wrong when it tends otherwise.'[6] He felt such a declaration was necessary because while he could see moral codes around him that dealt with relationships between individuals and relationships between individuals and society, 'there is as yet no ethic dealing with man's relation to land and the animals and plants which grow upon it.'[7]

Of course, the responsibility to care for the natural world is embedded in some of our oldest cultures – wisdom that became marginalised as agriculture industrialised. In Judaism, *tikkun olam* (literally 'repair of the world') is a concept defined by acts of kindness performed to perfect or repair the world. It is often used when discussing issues of social policy and safeguarding those who might be at a disadvantage, but in modern Jewish circles, *tikkun olam* has become synonymous with the notion of social action and the pursuit of social justice[8] – including environmentalism. '"*Olam*" or "world" comes from the same root as *hidden* so the repair we are asked to accomplish requires that we see the sacred hidden within the ordinary – that wholeness exists in all things, everywhere,' write John Wackman and Elizabeth Knight in their book *Repair Revolution*.[9] I spoke to Rabbi Albert Chait for his take on how *tikkun olam* relates to environmental regeneration. 'It's not just about correcting the wrongs of human behaviour,' he says. 'In Judaism, we believe that God gave us the world and then said to the people of the world, "look after it for me", so there's a sense of purpose. It sounds cheesy, but it's about doing the right thing. It also involves getting your hands dirty and it's about playing to your strengths, so that, hopefully, within any group of people, the world is put right.' He shares a quote with me from Rabbi Nachman – 'the day you were born is the day God decided the world couldn't function without you' – so there is a real sense of personal responsibility. And he tells a story about a man planting a carob tree that he wouldn't eat the fruit from because he wouldn't live long enough, which reminds me of the adage (variously described as an ancient Indian and Greek proverb and credited to everyone from Joycelyn Elders to Warren Buffett): 'Blessed are those who plant trees under whose shade they will never sit.' This is not just a metaphor – it comes from rural wisdom that dictated that each generation would replenish natural systems for the next.

And of course, an 'ethic dealing with man's relation to land and the animals and plants' has always been part of Indigenous belief systems. 'The word animism refers to something so commonplace... in Indigenous cultures, that most don't even have a word for it,' says Toko-pa Turner in *Belonging*.[10] 'It is the foundational belief that spirit and matter are one. That all things are imbued with a soul; not just humans and animals, but mountains, thunder, shadows, and even the wind.' When you believe everything has a soul, it is much harder to exploit it as a resource. And this is starting to be embedded into law, with the Ganges and its main tributary the Yamuna in India, and the Whanganui river in New Zealand all accorded the same status and legal rights as living human entities in 2017.[11]

In today's Western scientific worldview, humans are often set outside and above 'nature', our role either to control and coerce it into neat and tidy productivity or, if we decide it needs to be protected, to leave it well alone.[12] There is little space for mutually beneficial collaborations between humans and the more-than-human world. But Greg Kennedy makes a distinction between care that imposes its will on an external world of things and beings, and care that establishes a reciprocal relationship with what is cared for. 'Taking care of a thing in a way that lets it be what it is acknowledges, even if only tacitly, that the thing shares the same essential fragility of our own embodied existence,' he writes.[13] We don't need to 'save' nature – we need to understand the ways in which its vulnerabilities are entirely intertwined with our own. Every breath we take, every drop of water we drink, every mouthful of food we eat is utterly dependent on the natural systems we seem so set on destroying. We are not above nature, we are part of it – and this is something craftspeople have long understood.

In her book *Braiding Sweetgrass*, Robin Wall Kimmerer, botanist, professor and member of the Citizen Potawatomi Nation, shares research that she and graduate student Tom Touchet carried out, proving that black ash forests thrive when Potawatomi basket weavers harvest trees for their craft. In most of the sites they sampled, they found old trees and young seedlings, but hardly any trees in between. The saplings – the future of the forest – were dying or missing altogether. There were only two places they found saplings in abundance – where disease or storms had created a gap in the canopy and near communities of basket makers. 'Where the tradition of black ash basketry was alive and well, so were the trees,' she says, explaining that the saplings need the light created by gaps in the canopy, whether they are made by storms, disease or basket weavers. Wall Kimmerer found the same to be true of sweetgrass. Maps of historical locations of the grass show that the only places it still thrives are clustered around Native communities – particularly those known for their sweetgrass crafts. 'The grassy meadows tell us that, for sweetgrass, human beings are part of the system,' she says. 'A vital part.' The realisation that the Western industrialised world needs to mend its relationship with the natural world comes from some of the oldest communities on the planet – and in turn, their wisdom comes from nature. 'In Native ways of knowing, human people are often referred to as "the younger brothers of Creation",' says Wall Kimmerer. 'We say that humans have the least experience with how to live and therefore the most to learn – we must look to our teachers among other species for guidance.'[14]

Indigenous people comprise just 5% of the global population, but hold within their territories almost half of the world's remaining protected places, approximately 80% of the biodiversity and the largest carbon stores.[15] 'The Indigenous ways of knowing and being that European colonists saw as primitive and uncivilised are now being actively sought out to save our environment,' says Indigenous rights lawyer and executive director of the Land Peace Foundation, Sherri Mitchell Weh'na Ha'mu Kwasset. 'In recent years, scientists have realised that they are just now "discovering" what Indigenous peoples have long known.'[16] Experts from the United Nations, the scientific community, government agencies and environmental organisations are finally recognising that they will be key to addressing climate change.[17] But while industrialised countries must learn to centre historically marginalised wisdom, the responsibility cannot rest with Indigenous and rural communities alone. In their book *The Future We Choose*, Christiana Figueres and Tom Rivett-Carnac call for a 'deliberately regenerative Anthropocene'. They write: 'We will not have a regenerative Anthropocene by default, but we can create it by design... We will need artists as well as policy experts, farmers as well as leaders of industry, grandmothers as well as inventors, and Indigenous leaders as well as scientists.'[18] It is this coming together of worldviews that will make a difference – and, of course, craftspeople and remakers have their part to play.

Today's craftspeople are remaking those connections and working in collaboration with natural systems to create products that pass the stress test Figueres and Rivett-Carnac propose: 'Does it actively contribute to humans and nature living together as one integrated system on this planet?'[19] London-based designer Fernando Laposse (p. 188) works with Indigenous communities to champion traditional agricultural practices in his native Mexico, while providing income for farmers and craftspeople and encouraging biodiversity and future food security. When Sebastian Cox (p. 212) was studying, bamboo was touted as the ultimate renewable wood source. Looking closer to home, he developed a range of furniture made from coppiced hazel, the careful forestry of which promotes biodiversity in local woodlands. Gavin Christman (p. 206) is turning waste china clay into habitats for birds, bees and bats in urban environments, enabling humans to live in harmony with nature. And Sara Grady and Alice Robinson (p. 200) are creating a supply chain for leather that connects designers with its provenance and ensures full traceability and regenerative agriculture practices. These are all menders and remakers working in collaboration with nature. They understand that as humans we are part of the natural world and that we can exist in a way that is beneficial, restorative and regenerative to the more-than-human world.

Fernando Laposse

London-based Mexican designer Fernando Laposse (1988, Paris, France) grew up in Mexico, first visiting Indigenous family friends in the village of Tonahuixtla when he was six years old. Over the next eight years, he got to know the people, the food, the culture and the landscape. He moved to Paris at the age of 14 to study; when he came back a decade later, he barely recognised Tonahuixtla. 'The physical change in the landscape was immediately obvious,' he says. 'All the land was eroded.'

Fernando Laposse

The North American Free Trade Agreement (NAFTA) between Mexico, Canada and the United States came into force in 1994, opening the gates for America to sell Mexico their surplus grain at below-market prices, thereby undermining local production. In rural areas, instead of the companion or

Women of Tonahuixtla, Mexico, with the corn harvest

'three sisters' method of planting heritage corn together with beans and squash, North American corn was planted alone, creating a monoculture. Planting corn and beans together on mounds of earth with squash in between increases the soil temperature and improves drainage. The corn stalks provide a trellis for the beans to climb, the beans stabilise the corn in high winds and fix nitrogen in the soil, reducing the need for chemical fertilisers, while the wide leaves of the squash shade the ground, keeping the soil moist and helping to prevent weeds – all wisdom that has been passed down through the Indigenous community for generations, but which has only recently been endorsed by Western science.

Subject to selective breeding over 9,000 years, even natural corn is highly productive. If planted alone, it draws nitrogen out of the soil at unsustainable rates. On top of encouraging monocultures, the government-sponsored, genetically modified seeds were infertile, forcing Mexican farmers to buy new seeds every year, creating not only a dependency on costly chemical fertilisers but also on seed manufacturers. Debts piled up, the fields were abandoned and, with nothing growing on the land, the soil washed away in the rain. A reforestation programme was attempted, but the trees were unsuitable for the soil in its current state and simply withered away. This was the scene that Laposse returned to after ten years away from the village where he'd formed such happy childhood memories. 'This is happening all around the world,' says Laposse. 'But it's particularly tragic to see it in a village that is at the epicentre of corn history – Tonahuixtla is where corn was first domesticated.'

Laposse could see that the ecosystem that had protected this land for thousands of years was broken, and simply replanting

Laposse with farmers in Tonahuixtla, Mexico

heritage corn, beans and squash wasn't going to work. 'I started to think about agaves, because they were the only things still growing in the trenches left over from the failed tree-planting programme,' he says. 'What's so special about agaves is that they can basically grow on rocks, but as soon as they take root, they start to hold on to soil and create organic waste that becomes compost – they're pioneer plants.' He and his team worked out that they could plant rows of agave to hold the existing trench system in place – evening it out to effectively capture rainfall. As a result, rainwater would pool in the trenches long enough for it to soak into the parched soil instead of simply running off it. But they needed to create a market for the agave.

Laposse had previous experience of doing exactly this: he'd already created a new product using the waste products of heirloom Mexican corn farming – a colourful veneer material called Totomoxtle (pp. 192–195). To create this new craft, he worked with the community of Tonahuixtla, a small village of Indigenous Mixtec farmers and herders in the state of Puebla. The veneer showcases the full range of colours of the various corn species and has been used in high-end interiors all over the world – generating demand. This in turn provides additional income for farmers, and jobs for local women who make the veneers. But it's about more than using a waste product from food production; as well as preserving local biodiversity by supporting the farming of heritage species – many of which are endangered – it also promotes food security, because heritage corn produces fertile seeds. Laposse is working with the support of CIMMYT, the world's largest corn seed bank. Because these seeds have been bred for centuries in incredibly hot and dry conditions, there is hope that they might hold solutions for the climate challenges ahead. 'This is a project that exemplifies the power of design to transform, repair and promote social cohesion,' says Laposse. 'I am so glad that the concept of regeneration is finally becoming a mainstream idea. Yes, we create revenue from the leaves, but we've also gone to great lengths to reintroduce the seeds.'

He didn't need to invent a new material to make from agave, because one already existed. Agave yields a stiff fibre called sisal that has been used for centuries to make rope, as well as fishing nets and carpets – in fact, sisal is named after a port in Mexico from where it was traded. Sisal has largely been displaced by plastic, and its history is tainted with slavery and dangerous working practices, so Laposse felt a reinvention was in order. 'I went to visit a sisal workshop in southern Mexico, and the way they made rope was super-interesting,' he says. 'But what really captured my imagination was the moment just before they twisted it into a rope – it looked like hair.' He has created a series of 'hairy' sisal products, ranging from *Sisal Sanctum* (pp. 196–197) – a playful installation for the Citizen M hotel chain during the London Design Festival in 2018 – to slightly more practical items, such as benches called *The Dogs*, and he has done it ethically, with proper labour protections in place. 'It was important to do the whole procedure, from harvesting the plant to extracting the fibres and knotting them by hand,' he says. 'With this project, I hope to remind us that some of the answers to the environmental challenges of the future might be found in traditional crafts rather than exclusively in new technological discoveries.'

Ever since he returned to the village of his childhood, Laposse has dedicated himself to repairing its broken ecosystem. To date, he and his team have planted 70,000 agave plants, and they invest as much of their profit as they can (rather than restricting themselves to a fixed percentage) into planting more each year. As the agaves begin to repair the soil, new plants grow around them; these attract moths and bats that feed on pests that would normally attack the nearby corn, so there is less requirement for pesticides. Plus, the whole system retains rainwater, so the village wells are filling up again. And now, finally, the soil is ready for that reforestation programme. Another decade on and the village is once again starting to resemble his childhood memories and those of generations before him.

What's so special about agaves is that they can basically grow on rocks, but as soon as they take root, they start to hold on to soil and create organic waste that becomes compost – they're pioneer plants.

This is a project that exemplifies the power of design to transform, repair and promote social cohesion.

Totomoxtle is a veneer material made with husks of heirloom Mexican corn (above and opposite)

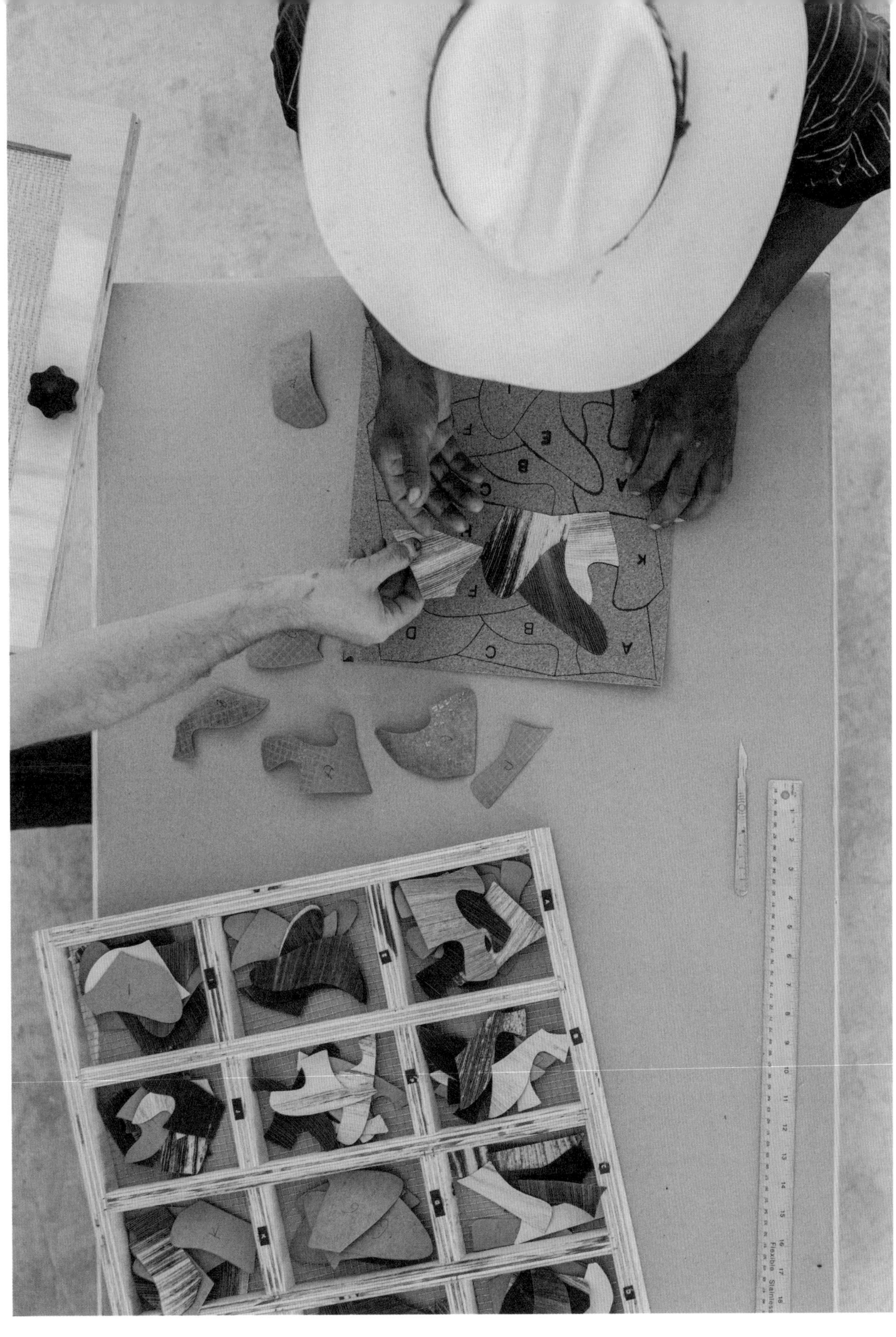

Totomoxtle Camo Table, heirloom corn husk marquetry on oak wood, 2020 (above and oppposite)

I hope to remind us that some of the answers to the environmental challenges of the future might be found in traditional crafts rather than exclusively in new technological discoveries.

Sisal Sanctum, an installation commissioned by citizenM, London, 2018

Sisal Monster, 2020 (above and opposite)

Sara Grady & Alice Robinson

Having completed a degree in womenswear, Alice Robinson (1993, Ellesmere, UK) started to question the work she was expected to put into the world as a fashion designer. 'I had become disillusioned by the pace of creating multiple "look collections" without feeling my designs had enough longevity or purpose to exist in the first place,' she explains. 'I didn't want to quit, but I did want to work out what my role as a designer was – in a world with enough stuff in it already.' She enrolled on the master's fashion programme at London's Royal College of Art and, rationalising that creating products with function, endurance and versatility might be the solution, decided to specialise in accessory design. This decision didn't dictate the use of leather, but leather's association with high-end fashion and its durable and versatile qualities made it the default choice. Despite having grown up in rural Shropshire among farmers and farm vets, until she began to work with leather, Robinson had never made a connection between the materials of her trade and the agriculture that provided the backdrop to her childhood. 'Looking at the material on my studio desk, for the first time I was struck by its anonymity, its lack of connection to its animal origins or beyond,' she says. 'My interest in regeneration grew as I began to grasp the globalisation of the leather supply chain and its deliberate disconnection from agriculture. I wanted to explore how my material choices were connected to other systems and, crucially, the people, places, land and animals behind them. I wanted to approach design in a way that wasn't extractive but was responsive and restorative of those broken connections.'

Sara Grady (left) and Alice Robinson at the finishers, producing British Pasture Leather

Asking questions about the provenance of the leather she was working with, Robinson found it impossible to get answers. 'The fact that a material so distinctly and inescapably connected to an animal – to a life – had no traceable history was in stark contrast to the provenance embedded in much of the farm produce I'd grown up around.' She decided that if she were going to make a collection, she would only work with raw materials that could be provided by a local farm. She created Collection 11458 (p. 204) from the wool and leather of a single sheep; the size of the collection representative of all that could be yielded from that one animal, using highly efficient pattern-cutting methods to minimise waste. The collection comprised a leather bag, woollen gloves and jumper, a leather card wallet and a pair of leather mules that had tiny offcuts of leather ground down and embedded into the soles. It was presented alongside 350 miniature burgers made from the meat of the same sheep – handmade by nose-to-tail chef Margot Henderson. The collection (minus the burgers) has since been acquired by the Victoria & Albert Museum in London.

After graduating, Robinson met a farmer who reared English Longhorn cattle. 'He passionately believed in feeding his local community in harmony with nature, using farming approaches that followed natural patterns, prioritising ecology and biodiversity, and by embedding provenance in his produce through full traceability. I followed him for a year from his farm to the local abattoir, and then I tried to follow the hide onwards all the way through to the production of leather.' But she discovered that the chain broke down between abattoir and tannery. The farmer used a small-scale abattoir that did not have a contract with a hide collector and, as a result, his hides were discarded. 'This was wasteful and disappointing on so many levels,' says Robinson. 'The collection

Sara Grady and Alice Robinson at the tannery, producing British Pasture Leather

I created as a result, Bullock 374, featured as a part of the V&A's exhibition *FOOD: Bigger than the Plate*.' As well as creating a collection of leather shoes, bags and accessories (p. 205), Robinson hosted a dinner with chef Sally Abé, during which guests were served the final cuts of Bullock 374. 'I hoped it would spark a curiosity and interest for designers to look beyond the natural materials and to the animal, place and community it had belonged to. The collection was the catalyst for me to create stronger connections between the farming and fashion communities; a fairer and regenerative food system dovetailing with the sustainability ambitions of the fashion and design communities.' Robinson realised that her experience with the English Longhorn cattle was far from unique. The hide is a significant part of an animal, but farmers don't receive any income from it and therefore often don't find out what happens to it. It makes up a part of what is called the 'fifth quarter' – from the Italian *quinto quarto*. When four-legged animals such as cows and sheep are slaughtered, butchery begins by dividing them into four 'quarters', each containing part of their body and one leg. The fifth quarter is everything else – including the hide, horns and bones. Often regarded as waste, it is de facto owned by the slaughterhouse, but typically sold on to different aggregators, and historically was an important source of revenue – it's also known as the 'butcher's profit'. However, because of the scale of today's meat and farming industries, hides and skins far exceed the demand for leather. Those from smaller practices are increasingly disposed of by the abattoir at a cost. Robinson knew she couldn't use all that leather single-handedly, so in 2020 she teamed up with Sara Grady (1975, New York, US) to create a new network for producing leather in the UK, utilising hides

I see our work as fitting into a broader movement of systems change.

from the farms whose regenerative practices they want to support, with the aim of giving designers and brands a choice when it comes to the leather they use.

'As a designer, it was frustrating that I was unable to source leather with knowledge of its origins on farms – and we wanted to create that opportunity, which led to Grady + Robinson and to producing British Pasture Leather,' she explains. They source hides exclusively from cattle raised on agroecological farms with Pasture for Life certification, which means their farming practices have positive impacts, such as soil carbon sequestration, biodiversity, land stewardship, animal welfare and resilient ecosystems. The pair purchase directly from the abattoirs and also give a cut to the farmers, giving the hides value beyond the traditional fifth quarter. 'Considering the care and resources that regenerative farmers invest in their livestock, hides are a valuable part of the herd,' says Grady. 'Once made into leather, the hide becomes the most enduring product of an animal raised for meat. Making meaningful use of the hide is a natural extension of a nose-to-tail culinary approach that fully values the animals we raise for food. Our supply allows farmers to see how their hides are being used, creating new connections around the products from the farms. The smaller-scale and local abattoirs that many of our partner farms use are integral to their production of local food with provenance. Bringing value to all parts of their animals supports the viability of these rural and regenerative businesses.'

Robinson and Grady work with UK tanneries, using a traditional vegetable tanning process and maintaining traceability through all stages of production. 'These trades and skillsets have withered in recent years, yet they are the linchpin in creating new systems for localised production and retaining a wealth of historic knowledge,' says Robinson. The enterprise is still nascent and the duo is immersed in creating new systems and fostering direct personal relationships along the way. 'The challenge is changing the perception of what this material can be: our goal is to create a beautiful and durable material that tells the story of the animal's life on land and builds discourse around the future of our food, farming and fibre systems,' says Grady. More than 70% of UK land is farmed. The patchworks of fields we take for granted as our 'green and pleasant land' increasingly comprise monocultural food 'factories'. Modern efficient farming methods are stripping the soil of nutrients, releasing carbon, and driving down biodiversity. We need to move to regenerative farming methods that prioritise people and planet as well as profit. Creating new systems for farmers that support the resilience of their businesses can contribute to a de-risking of that transition. 'I see our work as fitting into a broader movement of systems change,' says Robinson. 'A transitional approach to build meaningful collaborations across industries for the benefit of human and planetary health.'

Collection 11458, Alice Robinson, 2017

As a designer, it was frustrating that I was unable to source leather with knowledge of its origins on farms – I wanted other designers to have that opportunity.

Collection 374, Alice Robinson, 2019

Gavin Christman

Gavin Christman at the Green & Blue workshop

To explain why manufacturing, engineering and design are in his blood, Gavin Christman (1977, Stourbridge, UK) tells a story about his grandfather: 'He worked at a company called Midland Tube Products in the 1950s,' says Christman. 'It was part of a group called Tube Investments. One of their main competitors within that group was an American company that sent Midland Tube Products a very beautiful miniature tube showing off their engineering capabilities. Saying nothing, my grandfather and his team carefully constructed an even tinier tube, placed it inside the one they had received – and sent the pair back to the American firm.' It is a story about precision engineering, but it's also a story about quiet resistance to authority, which Christman seems to have inherited from his grandfather too. 'I've always wanted what I make to do the talking,'

Sparrow Block on a construction site

he says. 'What we do is not complicated, it's not cutting-edge, but it's got real purpose and that's what I'm most proud of.'

What he does – along with wife and co-founder Kate and a small team based in the Cornish seaside town of Perranporth – is to make habitats for solitary bees, birds and bats – 'products that help us all to make the changes necessary to protect our environment for future generations.' Modern houses and gardens lack the nooks and crannies that bees, birds and bats like to nest in, which means they are losing their habitats.

Having started their careers at Dyson, the couple was used to responding to client-led briefs, developed for the benefit of humans. 'We wanted to design for the unspoken client, for something bigger that doesn't necessarily have its own voice,' says Christman. 'When you set those sort of parameters, you know that you can't mess it up – this is really quite important stuff.'

Green & Blue, the company they founded, considers nature its primary stakeholder, so much so that when Christman heard new research from the RSPB at an international construction show where Green & Blue was launching its new sparrow terraces, suggesting that terraced nest boxes were not the best solution for the species, as previously believed, he pulled the product there and then. 'I got up and introduced the product as planned,' he says. 'But then made the statement that, in light of this new research, we would be going back to the drawing board to understand what the best thing is for the sparrow – and that's exactly

Bee Brick at the Chelsea Flower Show

what we did. The sparrows' needs had to come before those of our customers, our suppliers or even our balance sheet.'

You could argue that none of this is really regeneration – after all, the buildings are still going up, all Green & Blue is doing is making sure there is space for nature among all this human development. But Christman sees it differently: 'We are not separate from nature. If you stop talking for long enough and listen, it's right there – it doesn't matter if you're in a city, a five-acre garden or untouched wilderness. If you stop still for long enough, it's always in the background. What we're doing is making sure that we can coexist alongside – and actually listen to and learn from – nature, to ensure that we have a better, richer relationship with wildlife. You might only have a handkerchief garden, but as long as it's well planted, as long as you're considering where the sun rises and falls, and maybe including a small pond and a few bird boxes, it all adds up. All of our gardens add up to a decent amount of habitat.'

And it is all interconnected. According to the charity Buglife, one out of every three mouthfuls of the food we eat depends on pollinators. Bees are among the most important pollinators, and 90% of the UK's bees (some 224 species) are solitary. As their name suggests, solitary bees don't live in hives and they are not divided by role into queens, drones and worker bees, as are their hive-dwelling counterparts. Instead, they raise their young alone and, as they are only on the wing for a few weeks, the females have a short spell of time to find somewhere to lay their eggs. Mining bees dig holes in the ground, whereas cavity bees need to find a crack or crevice to nest in – which is where Green & Blue's Bee Bricks (above) come in. Cast from recycled aggregate from the Cornish china clay industry, they have tube-shaped nesting holes that are perfect for the egg cells, protective material, nectar and pollen that the female bee will layer inside. Leaf-cutter bees even plug the tube with a circular piece of leaf.

Bee Posts for solitary bees

As well as Bee Bricks, the company also makes Bee Pots, Bee Blocks, Bee Posts (above) and Bee Cells, alongside habitats for swifts, sparrows and bats. But they do more than just make the habitats, they also advocate for their primary stakeholder. They have worked hard to understand what the construction industry needs, making their Bee Bricks to the same specifications as a traditional brick so they are easy to fit, and pricing them in line with door fittings, so they are easy to justify. After decades of conversations, Brighton & Hove have recently become the first UK council to make them compulsory in all new-builds. No doubt, more councils will follow suit. 'There's an opportunity to create a real step change within construction,' says Christman. 'We might play a very small part in that; we might lead to bigger partners who can actually deliver the volume that might be required to see real change happen. But it takes courageous little businesses like Green & Blue to take those first steps.'

They have also introduced an annual 'solitary bee week' at the end of June, encouraging people to both 'wear their stripes' – wear striped clothes in solidarity with bees, to spread the word on social media – and 'earn their stripes' – pledge to undertake small actions such as planting wildflowers or creating a bare patch of soil for mining bees. 'We need to move, educate and mobilise more and more people from an earlier age to understand that the planet isn't just here to be taken from,' says Christman. 'It's something we need to listen to and learn from. We're not going to do that overnight – and I think that's the problem. It's too big a problem for one individual or one generation to solve. But there are huge opportunities with every generation to improve the status quo and move things forward. You've got to get on with it – you can't just sit around and wait to be told what to do.'

Leafcutter bee returning to a Bee Block with a piece of cut leaf

We wanted to design for the unspoken client, for something bigger that doesn't necessarily have its own voice.

A small Bee Block set among logs

A solitary bee capping a cell in a Bee Brick

Sebastian Cox

When designer and furniture maker Sebastian Cox (1986, Ashford, UK) was 12 years old, the charcoal burners came. ‘I can remember smoke hazing through the deforested landscape,’ he says. ‘It was a really vivid experience.’ They cut not just the woodland in which he grew up, but all the woodlands in the area, living in each one for a few weeks, burning the timber in kilns for charcoal before moving on to the next, so the effect stretched as far as the eye could see. But as striking as these scenes of seeming devastation were, what really stayed with the young Cox was how quickly everything grew back. By selectively felling trees, the woodsmen opened up the canopy, allowing more light to reach the forest floor and more species to flourish; being temperate hardwood, even the felled trees regrew from their root system without the

Sebastian Cox in his workshop

need for replanting. This was not destruction after all, but coppicing. This is a traditional woodland management practice that dates back thousands of years, which, according to Cox, mimics the conditions that mammoths would have once created by knocking down trees as they blundered through forests, and which beavers create when they bring down trees for their dams. Woodland species have evolved for such conditions over millennia, so this kind of management optimises woodlands for abundance and biodiversity. In fact, when woodlands are not managed in this way, they become 'overstood'; too many older trees block out the light required for new growth and the species that rely on it.

Today, Cox produces furniture based not on market demand, but on the timber that comes out of coppiced woodlands – including his own. 'I grew up understanding the cycle of coppicing and harvesting timber,' he says. 'During my design education at university, I became really interested in the idea of regeneration and using materials that are potentially inexhaustible. I was so excited by the idea that there was a material that would replenish itself without you doing anything other than harvesting it.'

The hewn products in Cox's Underwood collection (pp. 216–217) are made from coppiced hazel with the bark intact and feature slightly splayed legs and tapered feet. Each leg is tenon-jointed into a tabletop or seat made of English ash. Wooden furniture is often so highly processed that you could be forgiven for forgetting that it is made from trees. Not so this collection; the tapered hazel legs evoke evenings spent whittling sticks around a woodland campfire, or at least pencils sharpened with a knife. It provokes important questions about where materials come from and what happens to the environments from which they are taken – all questions Cox is more than happy to answer. The hazel is sourced from coppiced woodlands (his own and local woodlands managed in similar ways) and the ash is 'selectively felled', which means choosing trees to take down not only for their timber potential, but also to optimise the canopy – and therefore the amount of light reaching the forest floor – for biodiversity.

By the 13th century, most of the UK's woodlands would have been coppiced – and there would have been many more woodlands than there are today, but the Industrial Revolution brought about faster and cheaper ways of manufacturing the products once supplied from the woods by coppice workers. Coppicing – and woodlands – have been in decline ever since. Once woodlands become overstood, the timber becomes less valuable and is harder to remove without clearing them entirely. 'There is a gap between the conventional timber market that extracts with machinery only, and the traditional craft market, for which people extract the wood by hand and carry it out over their shoulders,' says Cox. This gap means that woodlands are either left alone to stagnate, or the timber is cleared and sold for firewood. This is something Cox is attempting to address with his Products of Silviculture collection, specifically designed to use larger-diameter timber. Coppiced timber takes approximately nine years to grow back to a useful size, so one in nine trees will be cut each year, until the woodland is back into coppiced management and rotation. The collection comprises chairs, desks, tables and sideboards made from British elm and coppiced birch, hornbeam, cherry and sweet chestnut, with slithers of bark left intact as a nod to their wilder days.

Cox has recently taken on a former agricultural building on the edge of a working farm on the Kent Downs, surrounded by 200 acres of woodland, in addition to his London workshop and family woodland. This facility, complete with sawmill and kiln for the machining and processing of timber at source, will enable his team to bring the woodland under management and give them end-to-end supply chain transparency. 'The industry isn't set up to allow people to work in the way that we want to work – no one is retailing coppiced wood for furniture making, for example,' says Cox. 'And the other advantage of working in this way is that we take full responsibility for our waste. Within our production process, we have grading stages to sort all the wood and we use anything that wouldn't make the grade for a tabletop or drawer front as drawer backs and sides. I quite like that secret reuse of what, in a more commercial system, would end up as waste. Even our wood chip gets used in our mycelium lights [p. 219].'

The stated mission on the Sebastian Cox website is twofold: to 'store 100 tonnes of CO_2 every year in adored items in people's homes, community spaces and workplaces' and to 'double the area of woodland and wild land in Britain by 2040, demonstrating how this incredible resource can be used, through advocacy and action'. It's about carbon and biodiversity and makes a lot of sense, but when I talk to him about his hopes for the future, his motivation is more personal. 'I want my daughters to know what a nightingale sounds like,' he says. 'It's existentially important to regenerate nature. Without functioning natural systems, the world as we know it ceases to operate, so on a high level, it's fundamental to our continued habitation of this planet. But we are only just starting to really understand the damage we have done, so I think it's essential that we not only try to make it habitable, and stay sustainable, but that we actually try to repair what has been lost. And I think that's a much more interesting, much more beautiful approach. My grandfather was raised in an environment where there were lots of nightingales – I want to make sure that my kids have the same opportunities. I want them to have a better opportunity to feel part of nature than I did in my childhood.'

I want my daughters to know what a nightingale sounds like.

Cox and his team operating the sawmill

I was so excited by the idea that there was a material that would replenish itself without you doing anything other than harvesting it.

Hewn items from the Underwood collection

A mycelium and timber stool

Mycelium and timber light shades

We are only just starting to really understand the damage we have done, so I think it's essential that we not only try to... stay sustainable, but that we actually try to repair what has been lost.

Notes

Page 2

1 Ayana Elizabeth Johnson & Katharine K Wilkinson, eds., *All We Can Save: Truth, Courage and Solutions for the Climate Crisis* (New York: One World, 2021), xxi.

Introduction – a case for paying attention

1 Adapted from https://dictionary.cambridge.org/dictionary/english/broken
2 www.kulturservern.se/wronsov/selfpassage. Accessed 25 December 2022.
3 https://www.metoffice.gov.uk/about-us/press-office/news/weather-and-climate/2022/red-extreme-heat-warning-ud
4 https://www.theguardian.com/uk-news/2022/jul/18/uk-transport-operators-say-worst-heatwave-problems-yet-to-come
5 https://www.theguardian.com/world/2022/jul/19/europe-heatwave-wildfires-death-toll-france-highest-temperatures
6 https://www.yesmagazine.org/opinion/2022/08/23/adrienne-maree-brown-endings
7 Steven J Jackson, 'Rethinking Repair', in Tarleton Gillespie, Pablo J Boczkowski and Kirsten A Foot, eds., *Media Technologies: Essays on Communication, Materiality, and* Society (Cambridge, MA: MIT Press, 2014), 221–222.
8 Jackson, 2014, 221–222.
9 Fred Rogers, better known as Mister Rogers, was the creator and host of the American preschool television series Mister Rogers' *Neighborhood*, which ran from 1968 to 2001. The quote is from him and was preceded by 'When I was a boy and I would see scary things in the news, my mother would say to me...'
10 Kate Fletcher, *Craft of Use: Post-Growth Fashion* (London & New York: Routledge, 2016), 101.
11 Christiana Figueres & Tom Rivett-Carnac, *The Future We Choose* (London: Manilla Press, 2020), 53.

Repair as restoration of function

1 *Compact Oxford English Dictionary*, 3rd edition (Oxford: Oxford University Press, 2005).
2 David Pye (1968), *The Nature and Art of Workmanship* (London and New York: Bloomsbury, 2015), 84.
3 https://www.etymonline.com/word/restoration
4 Quoted in Robin Wall Kimmerer (2013), *Braiding Sweetgrass: Indigenous Wisdom, Scientific Knowledge and the Teachings of Plants* (London: Penguin Random House, 2020), 9.
5 Lauren Chang speaking on podcast 'Circular with Katie Treggiden', season 2, episode 13, 2021. Available online: https://open.spotify.com/episode/3a35w1Aw2mniQRJYIFwMX-A?si=d0fd1e6a6466488d
6 With thanks to Tom van Dynein for introducing me to the concept of *open* and *closed* objects. Referenced in 'Circular with Katie Treggiden', season 2, episode 10, 2021. Available online: https://open.spotify.com/episode/2Ccdq9J8NQqgH-DZQWiDZQy?si=58334620a49749ab He was drawing on the work of Amy Twigger Holroyd – see Amy Twigger Holroyd, *Folk Fashion: Understanding Homemade Clothes* (London and New York: Bloomsbury, 2017), 128.
7 Pye, (1968) 2015, 84.
8 James Rebanks, *English Pastoral: An Inheritance* (London: Penguin, 2021), 82–84.
9 Dan Nosowitz, 'Farmers Demand Right to Fix Their Own Dang Tractors', *Modern Farmer*, 18 July 2016. Available online: https://modernfarmer.com/2016/07/right-to-repair/ Accessed 25 September 2020.
10 Nosowitz, 2016.
11 https://www.cnbc.com/2018/12/13/inside-apple-iphone-where-parts-and-materials-come-from.html
12 https://wccftech.com/apple-lobby-against-right-to-repair-bill/
13 https://univdatos.com/report/smartphone-repair-market/
14 https://time.com/4828099/farmers-and-apple-fight-over-the-toolbox/ Accessed 6 March 2023.
15 Tara Bahrampour, 'Have old broken stuff? These people will fix it for you – for free', *The Washington Post*, 15 January 2019. Available online: https://www.washingtonpost.com/lifestyle/2019/01/15/dont-throw-out-that-old-clock-these-folks-want-keep-it-ticking/ Accessed 28 April 2019.
16 Quoted in John Wackman & Elizabeth Knight, *Repair Revolution: How Fixers Are Transforming Our Throwaway Culture* (Novato, CA: New World Library, 2020), 93.
17 Quoted in Holroyd, 2017, 78.
18 https://www.theguardian.com/fashion/2017/jul/29/fashion-must-fight-scourge-dumped-clothing-landfill
19 Wackman & Knight, 2020, 92.
20 'Circular with Katie Treggiden', season 2, episode 8, 2021. Available online: https://spoti.fi/3tlyYmg
21 https://www.loc.gov/item/global-legal-monitor/2017-11-01/france-advocacy-group-files-criminal-complaint-against-alleged-planned-obsolescence-practices/
22 https://www.gov.uk/government/consultations/draft-ecodesign-and-energy-labelling-regulations-2021

Repair as storytelling

1 *Concise Oxford Dictionary*, 7th edition (Oxford: Oxford University Press, 1989), 881.
2 Quoted in Ralph Rugoff et al., *Kader Attia: The Museum of Emotion* (London: Hayward Gallery Publishing, 2019), 19.
3 Elizabeth Spelman, *Repair: The Impulse to Restore in a Fragile World* (Boston, MA: Beacon Press, 2002), 133–134.
4 Bonnie Kemske, *Kintsugi: The Poetic Mend* (London: Herbert Press, 2021), 12.
5 Richard Sennett, *The Craftsman* (London: Penguin, 2008), 200.
6 Bridget Harvey, *Repair-Making: Craft, Narratives, Activism*, PhD thesis (London: University of the Arts London, 2019).
7 https://www.hindustantimes.com/india/cambridge-expert-says-indian-jugaad-is-lesson-to-world/story-M3q6vFu8tEPj8eSNsAJo5M.html
8 'Patriotic Patches', in *Woman's Magazine*, 1941.
9 https://www.iwm.org.uk/collections/item/object/30016350
10 'Re-fashion for Spring', in *Vogue*, April 1946.
11 'Making Do', in *Woman's Magazine*, 1941.
12 'Home & Country Home Countries Edition', *Journal of the National Federation of Women's Institutes*, 1942, 24(4):62. Available in: Women's Library, London School of Economics, ref 5FWI/G/2/3.
13 Mass Observations (MO) Report 830 'Clothes Rationing', University of Sussex. Available online: http://ezproxyprd.bodleian.ox.ac.uk:3166/Documents/Details/FileReport-830 Accessed 19 January 2019.
14 'Royal Naval Slang & Terminology', HMS Ark Royal. Available online: https://arkroyal.net/index.php?option=com_content&view=article&id=24&Itemid=145 Accessed 5 September 2019.
15 Correct as of 19 November 2022: https://www.instagram.com/explore/tags/visiblemending
16 Katrina Rodabaugh, *Mending Matters: Stitch, Patch and Repair Your Favorite Denim and More* (New York: Abrams, 2018).
17 Kerstin Neumüller, *Mend & Patch: A Handbook to Repairing Clothes and Textiles* (London: Pavilion, 2019).
18 Nick Crossley, 'Social class', in Michael Grenfell (2008), ed., *Pierre Bourdieu: Key Concepts* (Durham: Acumen, 2011).
19 Pierre Bourdieu (1979), *Distinction: A Social Critique of the Judgement of Taste* (Cambridge, MA: Harvard University Press, 1984), 327.
20 Steven J Jackson, 'Rethinking Repair', in Tarleton Gillespie, Pablo J Boczkowski and Kirsten A Foot, eds., *Media Technologies: Essays on Communication, Materiality, and Society* (Cambridge, MA: MIT Press, 2014), 222.
21 Sasha Rabin Wallinger, 'Mottainai: The Fabric of Life, Lessons in Frugality from Traditional Japan', in *Textile Cloth & Culture* 10(3) 2012: 336–344. Available online: https://doi.org/10.2752/175183512X13505526963822 Accessed 27 July 2019.
22 Carol Hayes, 'Sashiko Needlework Reborn: From Functional Technology to Decorative Art', in *Japanese Studies* 39(1) 2019: 1–18. Available online: https://www.tandfonline.com/doi/pdf/10.1080/10371397.2019.1634978?needAccess=true Accessed 27 July 2019.
23 Hayes, 2019: 1–18.
24 Michael Taussig, 'Redeeming Indigo' in *Theory, Culture and Society* 25(3) 2008: 1–15. Available online: https://ezproxy-prd.bodleian.ox.ac.uk:7218/doi/abs/10.1177/0263276408090655 Accessed 7 August 2019.
25 Hayes, 2019: 1–18.
26 Rose Dahlsen, 'Turning Japanese', in *House & Garden*, 9 April 2014. Available online: https://www.houseandgarden.co.uk/article/boro-threads-of-life-somerset-house Accessed 30 July 2019.
27 Tatsuichi Horikiri, *The Stories Clothes Tell: Voices of Working-Class Japan* (London, Boulder, New York & Lanham: Rowman & Littlefield, 2016), 17, 10.
28 Reiko Wagoner, in Horikiri, 2016, introduction.
29 Horikiri, 2016, 7.

Repair as activism

1 https://dictionary.cambridge.org/dictionary/english/craftivism
2 Quoted in Ralph Rugoff et al., *Kader Attia: The Museum of Emotion* (London: Hayward Gallery Publishing, 2019), 86.
3 Quoted in Tal Fitzpatrick, *Craftivism as DIY Citizenship: The Practice of Making Change*, PhD thesis (Melbourne: University of Melbourne, 2018). Available online: https://minerva-access.unimelb.edu.au/handle/11343/219289?show=full Accessed January 2022.
4 Fitzpatrick, 2018.
5 Matt Ratto, *DIY Citizenship: Critical Making and Social Media* (Cambridge, MA: MIT Press, 2014).
6 Correct as of 2020: https://www.aidsmemorial.org/quilt
7 Marita Sturken, *Tangled Memories: The Vietnam War, the AIDS Epidemic and the Politics of Remembering* (Berkeley, Los Angeles & London: University of California Press, 1997), 186.
8 Bridget Harvey, *Repair-Making: Craft, Narratives, Activism*, PhD thesis (London: University of the Arts London, 2019), 46.
9 With thanks to Janet Gunter for making this connection for me. See our podcast interview for more: 'Circular with Katie Treggiden', season 2, episode 8, 2021. Available online: https://spoti.fi/3tlyYmg
10 Kat Lister, 'Anarchy in the UK: A brief history of punk fashion', in *Marie Claire*, 2015). Available online: https://www.marieclaire.co.uk/fashion/a-brief-history-of-punk-fashion-79145 Accessed 25 January 2022.
11 Quoted in Cheryl Buckley & Hazel Clark, *Fashion and Everyday Life: London and New York* (London and New York: Bloomsbury, 2017), 210.
12 Dick Hebdige (1979), *Subculture: The Meaning of Style* (London and New York: Routledge, 1991), 102.
13 Quoted in Rozsika Parker, *The Subversive Stitch: Embroidery and the Making of the Feminine* (London and New York: Bloomsbury, 2010), xix.
14 Fiona Hackney, 'Quiet Activism and the New Amateur: The Power of Home and Hobby Crafts', in *The Journal of the Design Studies Forum* 5(2) 2013: 169–193. Available online: https://www.tandfonline.com/doi/abs/10.2752/175470813X13638640370733
15 Sarah Corbett, *How to be a Craftivist: The Art of Gentle* Protest (London: Unbound, 2017), 22.
16 Quoted in Parker, 2010, xix.

Repair as healing

1 https://www.merriam-webster.com/dictionary/repair%20to & https://www.merriam-webster.com/dictionary/repair
2 John Wackman & Elizabeth Knight, *Repair Revolution: How Fixers Are Transforming Our Throwaway Culture* (Novato, CA: New World Library, 2020), 76.
3 Wackman & Knight, 2020, 76.
4 In current legal scholarship the restorative justice movement is described as 'based on a set of values that promoted healing, repairing harm, caring and rebuilding relationships among the victim, the offender and the community'. Elizabeth V Spelman, *Repair: The Impulse to Restore in a Fragile World* (Boston, MA: Beacon Press, 2002), 52.
5 Quoted in Wackman & Knight, 2020, 76.
6 Matthew B Crawford, *Shop Class as Soulcraft* (London: Penguin Books, 2009), 16–17.
7 Richard Sennett, *Together* (London: Penguin, 2012), 219.
8 Wackman & Knight, 2020, 14.
9 https://www.nhs.uk/mental-health/feelings-symptoms-behaviours/feelings-and-symptoms/loneliness-in-older-people/
10 Bridget Harvey, *Repair-Making: Craft, Narratives, Activism*, PhD thesis (London: University of the Arts London, 2019).
11 https://www.mentalhealth.org.uk/campaigns/unlock-loneliness/research-briefing
12 https://www.itv.com/news/2021-06-21/amazon-destroying-millions-of-items-of-unsold-stock-in-one-of-its-uk-warehouses-every-year-itv-news-investigation-finds
13 Janet Gunter speaking on podcast 'Circular with Katie Treggiden', season 2, episode 8, 2021. Available online: https://spoti.fi/3tlyYmg
14 https://sociologydictionary.org/agency/
15 Harvey, 2019, 232.
16 See note 12.
17 Harvey, 2019.
18 Quoted in Wackman & Knight, 2020, 81.

Regeneration as repair

1 https://dictionary.cambridge.org/dictionary/english/regeneration
2 Quoted in Robin Wall Kimmerer (2013), *Braiding Sweetgrass: Indigenous Wisdom, Scientific Knowledge and the Teachings of Plants* (London: Penguin Random House, 2020), 290.
3 https://ellenmacarthurfoundation.org/circulate-products-and-materials
4 https://wrightcfo.co.uk/2022/02/13/circular-economy/
5 https://www.etymonline.com/word/regeneration
6 https://www.aldoleopold.org/post/understanding-land-ethic
7 https://www.aldoleopold.org/post/understanding-land-ethic
8 Jennifer Noparstak, https://www.learningtogive.org/resources/tikkun-olam. Accessed 11 January 2022.
9 John Wackman & Elizabeth Knight, *Repair Revolution: How Fixers Are Transforming Our Throwaway Culture* (Novato, CA: New World Library, 2020), 94.
10 https://toko-pa.com/2020/06/30/belonging-as-an-ecosystem/
11 https://www.theguardian.com/world/2017/mar/21/ganges-and-yamuna-rivers-granted-same-legal-rights-as-human-beings
12 Wall Kimmerer, (2013) 2020, 163–164.
13 Quoted in Caitlin DeSilvey, *Curated Decay: Heritage Beyond Saving* (Minneapolis & London: University of Minnesota Press, 2017), 179.
14 Wall Kimmerer, (2013) 2020, 9.
15 Sherri Mitchell – Weh'na Ha'mu Kwasset, 'Indigenous Prophecy and Mother Earth', in Ayana Elizabeth Johnson & Katharine K Wilkinson, eds., *All We Can Save: Truth, Courage and Solutions for the Climate Crisis* (New York: One World, 2021), 19.
16 Mitchell – Weh'na Ha'mu Kwasset, 2020.
17 Mitchell – Weh'na Ha'mu Kwasset, 2020.
18 Christiana Figueres & Tom Rivett-Carnac, *The Future We Choose* (London: Manilla Press, 2020), 88.
19 Figueres & Rivett-Carnac, 2020, 89.

Photographic credits

Alun Callender
212

Anne Renwick
105

Aono Fumiaki
154, 155, 157, 158, 159

Antony Crolla
54

Athr Gallery
120, 121

Benn Berkeley
206, 207

Ben Peter Catchpole
161, 164, 165

Beth Davis
216, 217

Bouke De Vries
63, 65, 66, 67

Bridget Harvey
103

Bridget Smith
178, 179

Carmel King
77

Caroline Robinson, Lakeland Arts
106

David Stelfox
102

Fernando Laposse & Pepe Molina
188, 189, 190, 192, 193, 194, 195, 196–197, 198, 199

Frode Larsen, The National Museum of Art, Architecture and Design, Oslo, Norway
108-109

Green&Blue
209, 210, 211

Gundega Strauberga
30

Hannah Henderson
100, 101

Hannah Stanton
37

iceberg7
87

Jason Lowe – jasonlowe.eu
201, 202

Jim Bachor
172–173

John Domine
170–171

Jo Hounsome Photography
174, 175

Joshua Fray – joshuafray.com
204, 205

Keiko Matsui (www.keikomatsui.com.au). Photography by Ryo Yamauchi
68, 69, 70, 71, 72, 73, 74, 75

Khoogj
89, 90, 91, 92, 93

Kyle Ford
167

L.O.R.K
18, 19, 20, 22, 23

Lucy Emms
115, 116, 117

Lucy Willow – www.lucywillow.art
152, 153

Massimo Failutti
123, 125

Mark Blower
118, 119

Mark Campbell
176, 177

Martin Howse, 2022. CAST, Cornwall
150

Matthias Hoene
36

Michele Panzeri
58, 59, 60

Paul Scott
107, 110, 111

Paul Tucker
78–79, 82-83

Petr Krejci
218, 219

Raewyn Harrison
80, 84, 85

Ron Wetzel
168, 169

Roo Lewis
112

Rory Mulvey
98

Ruth Ward
39, 40, 41, 42, 43

Sam Bond
127 (right), 128–129

Sam Pearson
162

Stefan Paiu
215

Stephen King
180, 181

Sugru / FormFormForm Ltd
25, 26, 28, 29

Sylvain Deleu
131, 132, 133, 134, 135, 136

Tas Kyprianou
144

Tom Young
44, 45, 46

Vincent Dassi
31, 33, 34

Weiche Wu
124, 126, 127 (left)

Wrap London
160

Yeshen Venema
147, 148, 149

Acknowledgements

This book has been a long time in the making, so there are a long list of people to thank. I want to start with Celia Pym, who can be credited with sparking my interest in repair. When I saw her shortlisted work for the Women's Hour Craft Prize in the London's Victoria & Albert Museum in 2017, my initial reaction was 'what on earth is darning doing in a museum?' I have spent the last six years (and the best part of a master's) answering that question! My humble thanks to Claire O'Mahony, course director of the master's in the history of design programme at the University of Oxford, who supervised the dissertation in which I explored Celia's work and supported my initial explorations into many of the themes in these pages. My thanks also to the wider teaching team at Oxford: Charlotte Ashby, Anthony Buxton and Geoffrey Tyak – and of course to my cohort of fellow students (not least my partner in design crime, John Clegg) without whom I would not have survived the rigours of the programme!

I have known Jay Blades for a long time, but he is a very busy man these days, so I was delighted when he agreed to write the foreword – the icing on the cake was being described as his 'fairy godmother' – I'm just trying not to think about how old that means he thinks I am!

Talking to curators, artists, menders and remakers about repair is one of my favourite things to do, so I am incredibly grateful to the people profiled within this book – and to the other people I interviewed, not least Becky Sunshine, Kangan Arora, Carly Klineberg, Ellie Moseley, Daniel Charny and Rabbi Albert Chait.

I am eternally grateful to the small team of readers who offer unfiltered feedback on the early drafts of all my books – for this one, Lauren Chang and Bridget Harvey shared their wisdom and insights, adding nuance to my perspectives, deepening my lines of enquiry and saving me from multiple missteps – the same goes for my copy editing and proofing team, Anthony Leyton, Cath Phillips and my dad, Robert Treggiden. I want to thank Daniel Nelson and Sam Trenerry for their marketing support – and Madeleine Michell and the team at Toast, who let me road-test chapter excerpts on unsuspecting customers at their Brighton store.

The biggest thanks should probably go to Kirsty Spain who helps me keep the rest of my business on track when I slope off to write books – and to my husband Leyton Allen-Scholey who does the same for my home life! And finally, I am forever grateful to my publisher Ruth Ruyffelaere for believing in – and investing in – the idea for this book. I hope to reward that belief by proving Jay wrong and playing my part in making repair deeply and enduringly fashionable.

Colophon

Words & Concept
Katie Treggiden

Copy Editing
Anthony Leyton & Cath Phillips

Proofreading
Cath Phillips & Robert Treggiden

Graphic Design
Dylan Van Elewyck

Editor
Ruth Ruyffelaere

Printing
DZS Grafik

ISBN 978-94-9303-989-6
D/2023/6328/3

Printed and bound in Slovenia.
Published by Ludion.

Ludion
Zennestraat 34b
1000 Brussels, Belgium
info@ludion.be
www.ludion.be